Difficult People Decoded

Insights and Tactics for Improved Interpersonal Relations

Anita Patel

Table of Contents

INTRODUCTION 6

CHAPTER I: Identifying Difficult Personality Types 8

Introduction to various difficult personality types 8

Common traits and behaviors of difficult people 11

Self-assessment: Am I a difficult person? 13

CHAPTER II: The Narcissist's Playbook 17

Understanding narcissistic behavior 17

Signs of narcissism in relationships 20

Strategies for dealing with narcissists 23

CHAPTER III: The Drama Queen/King 26

Recognizing drama queens and kings 26

Coping with dramatic behavior 29

Reducing drama in your life 31

CHAPTER IV: The Control Freak 35

Characteristics of control freaks 35

Setting boundaries with control-oriented individuals... 38

Finding a balance in control dynamics 41

CHAPTER V: The Passive-Aggressive Personality 44

Identifying passive-aggressive behavior 44

Dealing with passive-aggressive tactics 48

Communication strategies to address passive-aggressiveness 51

CHAPTER VI: The Manipulator **55**

How manipulators operate 55

Protecting yourself from manipulation 58

Building assertiveness skills 60

CHAPTER VII: The Chronic Complainer **64**

Understanding chronic complainers 64

Responding to constant negativity 67

Encouraging positive change in complainers 69

CHAPTER VIII: The Victim Mentality **73**

Recognizing victim mentality 73

Supporting individuals stuck in a victim mindset 75

Promoting empowerment and resilience 78

CHAPTER IX: Difficult People at Work **82**

Dealing with difficult colleagues or bosses 82

Maintaining professionalism in challenging work
environments 85

Strategies for improving workplace relationships 88

CHAPTER X: Difficult People in Personal Relationships ... 93

Navigating difficult family members............................ 93

Handling difficult friends or partners 96

Strengthening personal relationships through
communication 99

CHAPTER XI: Self-Care and Boundaries **103**

The role of self-care in dealing with difficult people ... 103

Setting healthy boundaries 106

Maintaining your emotional well-being 109

CHAPTER XII: Conflict Resolution and Communication . 113

Effective communication techniques 113

Steps to resolve conflicts with difficult individuals 116

Building bridges and finding common ground 119

CHAPTER XIII: Growing Through Challenges 123

Personal growth opportunities in dealing with difficult people 123

Developing empathy and understanding 126

Becoming a more resilient and adaptable person 129

CONCLUSION **133**

INTRODUCTION

In a world brimming with diverse personalities, each interaction offers growth and connection opportunities. Yet, it's no secret that some individuals can prove to be challenging, testing our patience, empathy, and understanding. "Difficult People Decoded: Insights and Tactics for Improved Interpersonal Relations" is a comprehensive guide designed to empower you with the knowledge and strategies needed to navigate the complex terrain of human relationships.

Understanding and effectively dealing with difficult people is essential in both personal and professional life. Whether you encounter narcissists, drama queens, control freaks, or chronic complainers, this book will equip you with the insights necessary to decode their behaviors and the tactics required to foster better interactions.

This book delves into the intricate world of difficult personality types, offering practical advice, real-life scenarios, and actionable techniques to survive and thrive in challenging situations. Drawing from psychology, communication studies, and personal development, "Difficult People Decoded" is a roadmap for enhancing your interpersonal skills and promoting harmony in your interactions.

As we embark on this journey together, we'll explore the various dimensions of difficult people, learn how to set boundaries, and master the art of conflict resolution. Moreover, you'll discover the profound personal growth that can arise from these challenging encounters, ultimately emerging as a more compassionate, resilient, and adept communicator. So, let's embark on this enlightening expedition to decode the mysteries of difficult people and create stronger, more fulfilling relationships in the process.

CHAPTER I

Identifying Difficult Personality Types

Introduction to various difficult personality types

In our complex and interconnected world, the tapestry of human interaction is woven with many personalities. While these differences often enrich our lives and provide growth opportunities, they can also bring us face-to-face with individuals who are, to put it simply, difficult. Understanding the nuances of these difficult personality types is the first step toward surviving and thriving in such encounters. This section aims to introduce you to some of the most common and challenging personality types you may encounter in your personal and professional life, offering insights into their characteristics, behaviors, and potential strategies for effective interaction.

One of the archetypal difficult personality types is the Narcissist. Narcissists are characterized by excessive self-importance, a constant need for admiration, and a lack of empathy for others. They tend to be self-absorbed and manipulative and often exploit those around them to meet their own needs. Identifying a narcissist can be challenging, as they are skilled at presenting a charming and confident facade. However, beneath this veneer lies a fragile ego that is easily wounded, leading to defensive and often hurtful behaviors. To effectively interact with narcissists, it's crucial to maintain boundaries, avoid confrontation, and approach them with empathy and patience.

The Drama Queen/King is another challenging personality type that frequently disrupts relationships and situations with their exaggerated emotions and attention-seeking behavior. These individuals thrive on drama, often blowing minor issues out of proportion and creating turmoil where none is needed. Drama queens and kings can be exhausting to be around, as they monopolize conversations and drain the emotional energy of those in their vicinity. Dealing with them requires a delicate balance between empathy and assertiveness. While it's essential to acknowledge their feelings, it's equally important to set boundaries and encourage more constructive ways of expressing themselves.

Control Freaks are individuals who seek to exert dominance and control over every aspect of their lives, often at the expense of others' autonomy and well-being. They are meticulous and perfectionistic and struggle to delegate responsibilities. Control freaks can be micromanagers at work or overbearing partners in personal relationships. When dealing with them, it's essential to communicate openly and assertively, setting clear boundaries and expressing the need for collaboration rather than domination.

Passive-aggressive individuals are masters of indirect and subtle hostility. They may appear agreeable on the surface but then undermine or sabotage others behind their backs. Passive-aggressiveness can manifest in various forms, from sulking and giving the silent treatment to backhanded compliments and deliberate inefficiency. Confronting passive-aggressive behavior can be challenging, as these individuals often deny any wrongdoing. Effective communication is key, as it can help bring these hidden hostilities to light and promote more honest and direct interactions.

Manipulators use cunning and deceit to achieve their goals and control others. They excel at exploiting vulnerabilities and emotional weaknesses, leaving their targets feeling manipulated and used. Manipulative tactics may include guilt-tripping, emotional blackmail, or playing the victim. To deal with manipulators, it's crucial to maintain self-awareness and assertiveness. Recognize their tactics, set firm boundaries, and avoid getting entangled in their web of deception.

Chronic Complainers, as the name suggests, are individuals who habitually focus on the negative aspects of life and are quick to voice their grievances. They often see themselves as perpetual victims and rarely take responsibility for their circumstances. While it's essential to be empathetic and offer support to those going through difficult times, chronic complainers can drain the energy of those around them. Encouraging a shift toward a more positive mindset and constructive problem-solving can help mitigate their constant negativity.

Victim Mentality is a personality trait characterized by a perpetual sense of powerlessness and self-pity. Those with a victim mentality tend to blame external factors for their problems and often seek sympathy and attention from others. While empathy is crucial, it's equally important to encourage personal responsibility and empower individuals with a victim mentality to take control of their lives.

Each of these difficult personality types presents unique challenges in our interactions, but they also offer opportunities for personal growth and improved relationships. By understanding their behaviors and motivations, we can employ effective strategies to navigate these encounters with greater empathy, patience, and assertiveness. In the following chapters, we will delve deeper into each personality type, providing practical insights and tactics to help you decode and effectively interact with difficult people, ultimately leading to improved interpersonal relations in both your personal and professional life.

Common traits and behaviors of difficult people

In the intricate tapestry of human interactions, we encounter various personalities. While most interactions are harmonious and fulfilling, there are instances when we must navigate the challenging terrain of dealing with difficult people. These individuals exhibit a range of common traits and behaviors that make interactions with them a formidable task. Understanding these shared characteristics is vital to effectively managing and improving relationships with difficult personalities.

One of the hallmark traits among difficult people is a pronounced sense of self-importance. Whether dealing with a narcissist, a control freak, or a drama queen, you'll notice that they often prioritize their needs, desires, and opinions above those of others. This self-centeredness can manifest in various ways, from constantly interrupting conversations to insisting on having the final say in decisions. For these individuals, the world revolves around them, making it challenging to engage in a balanced and mutually satisfying relationship.

A common behavior exhibited by difficult people is a lack of empathy. Empathy involves the ability to understand and share the feelings of others, and it is a cornerstone of healthy relationships. On the other hand, difficult personalities struggle to connect with the emotions and experiences of those around them. For instance, a chronic complainer may dismiss your concerns while dwelling incessantly on their own, or a manipulator may exploit your vulnerabilities without regard for your feelings. This lack of empathy can leave you feeling unheard and undervalued.

Another shared characteristic is the tendency to engage in manipulative behaviors. Manipulation is a common tool in the arsenal of difficult individuals. Whether it's the passive-aggressive coworker who subtly undermines your efforts or the manipulative partner who uses guilt trips to get their way, these individuals are adept at getting what they want through cunning and deceit. Their manipulative tactics can be subtle and overt, but the end goal is to control the situation and those involved to their advantage.

Difficulty with handling criticism is a common trait among many difficult personalities. They often react defensively or with anger when confronted with feedback or constructive criticism. For example, a narcissist may respond to any form of criticism as a personal attack, while a drama queen may turn minor feedback into a full-blown emotional ordeal. This defensiveness can make addressing issues challenging and working towards resolutions healthily and productively.

Inconsistent or erratic behavior is another telltale sign of difficult people. Their moods and reactions can be unpredictable, making it difficult to anticipate how they will respond to different situations. For instance, a control freak may appear calm and composed one moment but explode in anger the next when things don't go their way. This unpredictability can create an atmosphere of tension and anxiety in relationships.

A common behavior among difficult individuals is blaming others or external circumstances for their problems. This behavior is often seen in those with a victim mentality, who habitually view themselves as powerless victims of circumstances beyond their control. They rarely take responsibility for their actions or seek solutions to their problems. Instead, they rely on others to provide sympathy and support, perpetuating a cycle of helplessness.

One more shared characteristic is a propensity for drama and conflict. Drama queens and kings, in particular, thrive on stirring up emotional turmoil and creating unnecessary conflicts. They may exaggerate minor issues, engage in gossip, or constantly seek attention to feed their need for drama. This behavior can be draining for those around them and can disrupt the harmony of relationships and environments.

Finally, difficult individuals often struggle with communication skills. Effective communication is essential for resolving conflicts, building trust, and maintaining healthy relationships. However, many difficult personalities cannot express themselves clearly, listen actively, or engage in open and honest dialogue. This communication barrier can lead to misunderstandings, frustration, and escalating conflicts.

While these common traits and behaviors may seem challenging to navigate, it's essential to recognize that difficult people often exhibit these characteristics due to their own insecurities, fears, and past experiences. Understanding the root causes of their behavior can help you approach them with empathy and patience. In the following chapters, we will explore specific strategies and tactics for effectively dealing with each type of difficult personality, aiming to improve your interpersonal relations and foster more harmonious interactions in both your personal and professional life.

Self-assessment: Am I a difficult person?

To understand and effectively deal with difficult people, it's essential to begin by turning the spotlight inward and engaging in an honest self-assessment. This self- reflection process involves examining our own behaviors, attitudes, and characteristics to determine whether we, too, may exhibit traits associated with being a difficult person. Acknowledging and addressing these tendencies is critical to improving our interpersonal relationships and fostering healthier interactions with others.

One of the key indicators of being a difficult person is a lack of self-awareness. Self-awareness involves the ability to recognize and understand our own thoughts, emotions, and behaviors. Difficulty in self-assessment often stems from a failure to acknowledge our flaws, biases, and their impact on those around us. If we consistently find ourselves dismissing feedback, deflecting blame, or being resistant to self-improvement, it may be a sign that we are not as self-aware as we should be.

Another sign to watch out for is an inability to empathize with others. Empathy is the capacity to understand and share the feelings of others, and it plays a crucial role in building and maintaining healthy relationships. A lack of empathy can manifest as indifference or insensitivity to the emotions and needs of those around us. If we frequently disregard others' feelings, dismiss their concerns, or prioritize our own needs without regard for theirs, it's an indication that our empathetic capacity may be underdeveloped.

Difficulty in accepting feedback or criticism is another telltale sign of being a difficult person. When others offer constructive criticism or express their concerns about our behavior, do we react defensively or become dismissive? Being open to feedback and willing to improve is essential for personal growth and maintaining positive relationships. It may be time to examine our response patterns if we consistently resist feedback or engage in arguments and excuses when confronted with our shortcomings.

A tendency to dominate conversations and center discussions around ourselves can also indicate being difficult. Healthy interactions involve a balanced exchange of ideas, thoughts, and feelings. However, if we find ourselves consistently monopolizing conversations, interrupting others, or making every discussion about our experiences or opinions, we may inadvertently alienate those around us.

Difficulty in managing emotions is another trait commonly associated with being a difficult person. This can manifest as frequent mood swings, explosive anger, or excessive negativity. Emotional intelligence, which includes regulating our emotions and responding to situations with composure, is a fundamental aspect of healthy interpersonal relations. If we struggle to control our emotions, often allowing them to dictate our behavior and reactions, it can strain our interactions with others.

Another behavior to consider is whether we engage in manipulative tactics. Manipulation involves using cunning and deceit to achieve our goals or control others. It can take various forms, such as guilt-tripping, emotional blackmail, or playing the victim. If we find ourselves resorting to manipulation to get our way or influence others, it clearly indicates that we may be exhibiting difficult behavior.

Chronic complaining is yet another behavior that can cast us in the role of a difficult person. Constantly focusing on the negative aspects of life and venting our grievances without seeking solutions or positivity can be draining for those around us. While it's essential to express our concerns and feelings, doing so in a way that perpetuates a cycle of negativity can harm our relationships.

A lack of accountability for our actions is critical to consider in self-assessment. Difficult people often avoid taking responsibility for their behavior and its consequences. If we frequently blame external factors, circumstances, or other people for our problems without acknowledging our role, we may inadvertently cultivate a difficult persona.

Lastly, consider whether you create unnecessary drama and conflict in your relationships. Do you escalate minor issues into major confrontations? Do you thrive on stirring up emotional turmoil? Drama and conflict can be disruptive and harmful to relationships, and if we consistently contribute to them, it's a sign that we may be part of the problem.

It's important to note that self-assessment is not about self-condemnation but about self-improvement and personal growth. Recognizing areas where we may exhibit difficult behavior is the first step toward positive change. Self-awareness and a willingness to address these tendencies can lead to improved relationships, enhanced emotional intelligence, and greater overall well-being.

If, upon reflection, you recognize that you exhibit some of these difficult behaviors, don't despair. Change is possible, and personal growth is a lifelong journey. Seeking support through therapy, self-help resources, or open communication with trusted friends and family members can be invaluable in your quest to become a more empathetic, self-aware, and emotionally intelligent individual. Remember that self-assessment is a powerful tool for transformation, and by taking this step, you are already on the path to becoming a better version of yourself and fostering healthier, more harmonious relationships with those around you.

CHAPTER II

The Narcissist's Playbook

Understanding narcissistic behavior

Narcissism, a term rooted in Greek mythology, refers to excessive self-love and an inflated sense of one's own importance. When we discuss narcissistic behavior in the context of individuals, we are referring to a personality trait characterized by an exaggerated sense of self-importance, a constant need for admiration, and a lack of empathy for others. Understanding narcissistic behavior is essential not only for identifying narcissists but also for effectively interacting with them, setting boundaries, and protecting your own well-being.

At the core of narcissistic behavior lies an excessive and fragile ego. Narcissists often harbor deep-seated insecurities and fears of inadequacy beneath their confident facade. They construct an elaborate self-image built on grandiosity and self-importance to compensate for these vulnerabilities. They believe they are exceptional, unique, and entitled to special treatment and attention. This grandiose self-perception is a key driver of their behavior.

One of the defining features of narcissistic behavior is the constant need for admiration and validation. Narcissists thrive on attention and praise and are driven by an insatiable desire for external affirmation. They seek admiration from their friends, family, colleagues, and society at large. This need for validation often leads them to engage in attention-seeking behaviors, whether through boasting, self-promotion, or seeking out situations where they can bask in the spotlight.

While narcissists may appear confident and self-assured on the surface, their behavior is often a facade masking a deep sense of insecurity. This vulnerability is especially evident in their reaction to criticism or perceived slights. Narcissists are extremely sensitive to criticism, which they interpret as a direct attack on their self-worth. In response, they can become defensive, hostile, or even enraged. Their inability to accept feedback or admit fault can strain relationships and hinder personal growth.

A hallmark of narcissistic behavior is a lack of empathy. Empathy involves the capacity to understand and share the feelings of others, and it is a fundamental building block of healthy relationships. Narcissists, however, struggle to connect with the emotions and experiences of those around them. They often view others as tools or extensions of themselves, with their needs and feelings taking precedence. This lack of empathy can result in insensitive or callous behavior, as they prioritize their own desires and agendas without regard for the impact on others.

Manipulation is another crucial aspect of narcissistic behavior. Narcissists are skilled at manipulating others to meet their own needs and desires. They may employ tactics such as guilt-tripping, gaslighting, or emotional blackmail to control and influence those around them. Their manipulative behavior often maintains their grandiose self-image and secures the admiration and attention they crave.

It's important to note that narcissistic behavior exists on a spectrum. While some individuals may display occasional narcissistic traits, others meet the criteria for Narcissistic Personality Disorder (NPD), a more severe and pervasive condition. NPD is characterized by a consistent pattern of narcissistic behavior that significantly impairs one's functioning and relationships.

Understanding narcissistic behavior is crucial not only for recognizing it in others but also for navigating interactions with narcissists. When dealing with narcissists, it's essential to set clear boundaries and communicate assertively. While they may push back against these boundaries, maintaining your own self-respect and asserting your needs is vital for protecting your well-being.

Furthermore, it's essential to resist the temptation to engage in power struggles or arguments with narcissists. Their defensiveness and unwillingness to admit fault can make such interactions fruitless and emotionally exhausting. Instead, focusing on your own emotional health and self-care is often a more productive use of your energy.

Empathy can be a powerful tool when dealing with narcissistic individuals. While they may lack empathy themselves, demonstrating understanding and empathy toward them can help de-escalate conflicts and potentially lead to more constructive interactions. However, balancing empathy and assertiveness is essential to avoid being manipulated or mistreated.

In some cases, seeking professional help, such as therapy or counseling, may be necessary when dealing with narcissistic behavior, especially when it significantly impacts your mental and emotional well-being. Therapists can guide you in managing difficult relationships and developing coping strategies.

In conclusion, understanding narcissistic behavior is essential for recognizing it in others and effectively managing interactions with narcissists. It involves recognizing their excessive self-importance, constant need for admiration, lack of empathy, and manipulative tendencies. While navigating relationships with narcissists can be challenging, setting boundaries, practicing empathy, and prioritizing self-care are essential strategies for protecting your own well-being in such encounters. By understanding the roots of narcissistic behavior and its impact, you can develop strategies to mitigate its effects and promote healthier interactions in your personal and professional life.

Signs of narcissism in relationships

Narcissism, a personality trait characterized by an exaggerated sense of self-importance, a constant need for admiration, and a lack of empathy for others, can profoundly impact interpersonal relationships. While not everyone who exhibits narcissistic traits has Narcissistic Personality Disorder (NPD), understanding the signs of narcissism in relationships is crucial for recognizing potential challenges and navigating them effectively.

One of the most prominent signs of narcissism in relationships is an excessive need for attention and admiration. Narcissists often demand constant praise and validation from their partners, seeking reassurance of their exceptional qualities and worth. They may fish for compliments, dominate conversations, or expect their needs to precede everything else. This insatiable desire for admiration can leave their partners feeling emotionally drained and neglected.

Narcissists often display an exaggerated sense of entitlement. They believe they deserve special treatment, regardless of whether it's warranted or fair. In relationships, this entitlement can manifest as an expectation that their partners should cater to their every whim, meet their needs at all times, and prioritize their desires above all else. This can create an unbalanced dynamic, where the narcissist's wishes consistently take precedence.

Another sign of narcissism in relationships is a lack of empathy. Empathy, the ability to understand and share the feelings of others, is a cornerstone of healthy relationships. Narcissists, however, struggle to connect with their partner's emotions and experiences. They may dismiss their partner's concerns, be insensitive to their feelings, or fail to offer support during difficult times. This lack of empathy can lead to emotional neglect and hurt in the relationship.

Manipulative behavior is a common feature of narcissistic individuals. Narcissists use cunning tactics to achieve their goals and control their partners. This can include emotional manipulation, such as guilt-tripping, gaslighting, or playing the victim. Manipulative behavior is often driven by the narcissist's need to maintain their grandiose self-image and secure the admiration and attention they crave.

In relationships, narcissists may also display a tendency to idealize and devalue their partners. Initially, they may put their partner on a pedestal, showering them with affection and admiration. This idealization phase can be intense and captivating. However, it is often followed by a devaluation phase, during which the narcissist becomes critical, dismissive, or emotionally distant. This cycle of idealization and devaluation can leave their partners feeling confused, hurt, and constantly seeking their approval.

Another sign of narcissism in relationships is a tendency to deflect blame and avoid responsibility. When conflicts or problems arise, narcissists often refuse to acknowledge their own role in the issue. Instead, they may shift blame onto their partners or external circumstances, deflecting any criticism away from themselves. This behavior can hinder effective communication and conflict resolution in the relationship.

Narcissists may also engage in competitive behaviors within the relationship. They view relationships as a power struggle, always seeking to assert dominance and maintain control. This competitive mindset can manifest as needing to "win" arguments, always be right, or constantly trying to outdo their partner. Such behaviors can create a hostile and combative atmosphere in the relationship.

Furthermore, narcissists may lack boundaries in their relationships. They may invade their partner's personal space, disregard their partner's need for privacy, or consistently overstep boundaries without remorse. This lack of respect for personal boundaries can lead to feelings of violation and discomfort in the relationship.

In addition to these signs, narcissists often exhibit a high degree of superficial charm and charisma. They can be charismatic and persuasive, drawing people in with their confident and engaging demeanor. However, this charm is often a mask that hides their underlying narcissistic traits.

It's important to note that narcissism exists on a spectrum. While some individuals may display occasional narcissistic traits, others meet the criteria for Narcissistic Personality Disorder (NPD), a more severe and pervasive condition. NPD is characterized by a consistent pattern of narcissistic behavior that significantly impairs one's functioning and relationships.

Recognizing the signs of narcissism in a relationship is the first step toward effectively dealing with the challenges it presents. Setting boundaries, practicing assertive communication, and seeking support from friends, family, or a therapist can be essential strategies for maintaining your well-being in a relationship with a narcissist. Understanding that narcissistic behavior is rooted in insecurity and the need for validation can also help you approach the relationship with empathy and patience. Ultimately, while narcissism can be challenging to navigate, awareness and effective strategies can lead to healthier and more balanced relationships.

Strategies for dealing with narcissists

Navigating relationships with narcissists can be a complex and challenging endeavor. Their behavior, characterized by an exaggerated sense of self-importance, a constant need for admiration, and a lack of empathy for others, often creates turmoil and tension in interpersonal interactions. However, there are strategies you can employ to effectively deal with narcissists while protecting your own well-being and maintaining healthy boundaries.

One of the first and most crucial strategies is setting clear boundaries. Narcissists tend to disregard personal boundaries, often intruding into your personal space and disregarding your need for privacy. Establishing and maintaining firm boundaries is essential for safeguarding your emotional and mental well-being. Be explicit about your limits, and assertively communicate when those boundaries are crossed. While narcissists may push back against these boundaries, maintaining your own self-respect and asserting your needs is vital.

Maintain your sense of self-worth and self-esteem.

Narcissists can be skilled at eroding their partner's self-confidence and self-esteem through criticism, belittling comments, or manipulation. To counteract this, it's essential to cultivate a strong sense of self-worth and self-respect. Remind yourself of your strengths, achievements, and positive qualities. Seek support from friends, family, or a therapist to bolster your self-esteem and resilience.

Recognize that narcissists thrive on attention and validation. They have an insatiable need for admiration and often employ attention-seeking behaviors to fulfill this need. It's crucial to avoid feeding into this cycle by refusing to provide excessive attention or praise. Instead, offer constructive feedback and limit compliments to genuine instances of achievement or positive behavior.

Practice assertive communication. When addressing issues with a narcissist, it's important to communicate assertively, expressing your needs, feelings, and boundaries clearly and respectfully. Avoid aggressive or passive-aggressive communication, as these can escalate conflicts. Stay calm and composed, and focus on the issue at hand rather than engaging in personal attacks or character assassinations.

Avoid power struggles and arguments. Narcissists often resist admitting fault or accepting criticism, leading to unproductive arguments. It's important to recognize when engaging in power struggles is futile and instead prioritize your own emotional well-being. Choose your battles wisely and be prepared to disengage from unproductive discussions.

Maintain a support network. Dealing with a narcissist can be emotionally taxing, so it's essential to have a support network in place. Friends, family, or a therapist can provide emotional support, validation, and guidance as you navigate the challenges of the relationship. Sharing your experiences with trusted individuals can help you gain perspective and maintain your mental and emotional resilience.

Set realistic expectations. Recognize that changing a narcissist's behavior is challenging, and they may not be receptive to change. It's essential to set realistic expectations for the relationship and accept that you may not be able to change the narcissist. Focus on what you can control—your reactions, boundaries, and self-care.

Avoid personalizing their behavior. Narcissists often exhibit erratic and hurtful behavior, but it's important to remember that their actions reflect their insecurities and needs, not a commentary on your worth or value. Avoid personalizing their behavior and instead view it through the lens of their narcissistic traits.

Consider professional help. In some cases, seeking professional help, such as couples therapy or individual counseling, can be beneficial when dealing with a narcissist. A skilled therapist can guide on improving communication, setting boundaries, and managing conflicts within the relationship.

Practice self-care. Dealing with a narcissist can be emotionally draining, so it's crucial to prioritize self-care. Engage in activities that bring you joy and relaxation, maintain a healthy lifestyle, and seek relaxation techniques or mindfulness practices to manage stress. Prioritizing your well-being is essential for maintaining resilience in challenging relationships.

Detach emotionally when necessary. If the relationship becomes too toxic or damaging to your well-being, it may be essential to consider detaching emotionally or, in extreme cases, ending the relationship. Recognize when the negative impact on your mental and emotional health outweighs any potential benefits of the relationship and prioritize your own well-being.

Understanding that dealing with a narcissist can be an ongoing and challenging process is essential. It's unlikely that a narcissist will undergo significant personality changes, and it's necessary to manage your expectations accordingly. Your focus should be on maintaining your own emotional health, asserting your boundaries, and employing effective communication strategies to minimize conflict and protect your well-being. By implementing these strategies and seeking support when needed, you can navigate relationships with narcissists more effectively while preserving your own mental and emotional resilience.

CHAPTER III

The Drama Queen/King

Recognizing drama queens and kings

Drama queens and kings, we all know them. These individuals have an uncanny ability to turn the most straightforward situations into extravagant productions. Whether it's a minor inconvenience or a personal triumph, drama queens and kings are always at the forefront, seeking attention and validation. In this section, we will explore the characteristics that define these individuals, their impact on relationships and environments, and strategies for recognizing and dealing with them effectively.

One of the key characteristics of drama queens and kings is their constant need for attention. They thrive on being the center of the spotlight and will go to great lengths to ensure they are noticed. It's common for them to exaggerate their emotions and reactions to draw attention to themselves. For instance, a drama queen may turn a minor disagreement into a full-blown argument, complete with tears and loud outbursts, while a drama king might make a small accomplishment sound like a monumental achievement. Their need for attention often leads to them monopolizing conversations and making everything about them, leaving little room for others to express themselves.

Another hallmark trait of drama queens and kings is their tendency to create and amplify conflicts. They are skilled at stirring the pot and fueling drama in any situation. They may gossip, spread rumors, or twist stories to incite drama, often pitting people against each other for their amusement or to maintain their position as the focal point. This constant drama can be exhausting for those around them, creating an atmosphere of tension and unease.

Furthermore, drama queens and kings often lack emotional regulation. Their reactions to everyday situations are often disproportionate to the circumstances. A minor setback may lead to tears and despair, while a minor success can result in boastful and over-the-top celebrations. This lack of emotional control can make it challenging to have stable and harmonious relationships with them, as their unpredictable emotional rollercoaster can be draining for those trying to maintain a sense of balance.

In addition to their emotional volatility, drama queens and kings tend to have a self-centered perspective. They are primarily concerned with their own needs, desires, and feelings, often disregarding the needs and feelings of others. Empathy and understanding are often in short supply when dealing with these individuals, as they are preoccupied with their own narratives and desires. This self-absorption can be frustrating for those trying to have meaningful and reciprocal relationships.

Recognizing drama queens and kings is crucial because their behavior can significantly impact relationships and environments. In personal relationships, their constant need for attention and emotional turmoil can be draining and exhausting for partners, friends, and family members. It can create a sense of instability and insecurity, as individuals may never know what to expect from them. Workplace environments can also suffer when drama queens and kings are present. Their penchant for stirring up conflicts and seeking attention can disrupt productivity, create workplace tension, and damage team dynamics.

So, how can we recognize and deal with drama queens and kings effectively? Firstly, it's essential to trust your instincts. If someone consistently seeks attention, exaggerates their emotions, and creates unnecessary drama, they may fall into this category. Observing patterns of behavior and reactions over time can help confirm your suspicions. Secondly, set boundaries. Clearly communicate your expectations for respectful and balanced interactions. Let them know that excessive drama is unacceptable and will not be tolerated.

Moreover, practice empathy and understanding. While it can be challenging to connect with drama queens and kings, recognizing that their behavior may stem from their own insecurities and need for validation can help you approach them with more compassion. Encourage open and honest communication, and try to steer conversations away from constant self-centered narratives.

In some cases, seeking professional help may be necessary. If you find that a drama queen or king's behavior is causing significant distress in your life or their own, suggesting therapy or counseling can be helpful. A trained therapist can assist them in addressing underlying emotional issues and developing healthier coping mechanisms.

In conclusion, recognizing drama queens and kings is essential for maintaining healthy relationships and environments. These individuals thrive on attention, create unnecessary conflicts, and often lack emotional regulation. Their behavior can be draining and disruptive, but with proper awareness and strategies, we can navigate these relationships more effectively. By setting boundaries, practicing empathy, and seeking professional help when needed, we can minimize the impact of drama queens and kings on our lives and promote more balanced and harmonious interactions.

Coping with dramatic behavior

Dealing with dramatic behavior can be a challenging and emotionally draining experience. Dramatic behavior can disrupt relationships and create unnecessary stress, whether it's a friend, family member, colleague, or even oneself. This section will explore strategies for coping with dramatic behavior, both when others exhibit it and when we find ourselves caught in its grip.

First and foremost, it's essential to remain calm and composed when confronted with dramatic behavior. When someone around us is being overly emotional or seeking attention through dramatic displays, it can be tempting to react with frustration or irritation. However, responding with anger or impatience only fuels the drama and escalates the situation. Instead, take a deep breath and try to maintain a sense of emotional stability. This will help you stay grounded and serve as a model for the dramatic individual, showing them a more balanced way of dealing with emotions.

Empathy is another powerful tool for coping with dramatic behavior. While it may be challenging to understand why someone behaves dramatically, taking a moment to put yourself in their shoes can be enlightening. Try to see the situation from their perspective and consider what might be driving their behavior. Often, dramatic individuals seek validation, attention, or relief from their inner turmoil. Recognizing their underlying needs can help you respond with compassion rather than judgment.

Setting clear boundaries is crucial when dealing with dramatic behavior. Let the individual know what behavior is acceptable and what is not. Calmly and assertively communicate your expectations for respectful interactions. For example, you might say, "I am here to listen and support you, but I cannot engage in a conversation when you're yelling or making exaggerated claims." Enforcing these boundaries consistently can help establish a healthier dynamic in your relationship and discourage dramatic outbursts.

Active listening is a valuable skill when coping with dramatic behavior. Often, individuals resort to dramatic displays because they feel unheard or misunderstood. By actively listening and validating their feelings, you can de-escalate the situation and create a safe space for them to express themselves. Ask open-ended questions and offer empathetic responses to show your interest in their perspective.

Self-care is essential when dealing with dramatic behavior, especially if you are closely related to a dramatic person. Constantly absorbing their emotional turbulence can take a toll on your well-being. Make sure to prioritize your own mental and emotional health by engaging in activities that bring you joy and relaxation. Setting aside time for self-reflection and personal growth can also help you maintain your own emotional balance in the face of drama.

Sometimes, it may be necessary to seek professional help when dealing with dramatic behavior. If the dramatic behavior is causing significant distress in your life or the individual's life displaying it, therapy or counseling can be a valuable resource. A trained therapist can help both parties explore the underlying causes of the behavior and develop healthier coping mechanisms. They can also facilitate productive communication and conflict resolution strategies.

Self-awareness is critical to making positive changes when you exhibit dramatic behavior. Take a step back and reflect on your actions and reactions. Ask yourself why you are reacting in such an intense manner. Are you seeking attention, validation, or relief from inner turmoil? Identifying the root causes of your dramatic behavior is the first step toward addressing it.

Once you have identified the underlying issues, work on developing healthier coping mechanisms. This may involve learning to express your emotions more balanced and constructively. Journaling, meditation, or seeking support from a therapist can all be effective tools for managing intense emotions and reducing the impulse to engage in dramatic displays.

Taking responsibility for your actions and their impact on others is also essential. Apologize if your dramatic behavior has hurt or alienated someone. Acknowledging the effect of your actions and expressing genuine remorse can go a long way in repairing damaged relationships.

In conclusion, coping with dramatic behavior requires patience, empathy, self-care, and effective communication. Whether you are dealing with a dramatic person in your life or working on managing your own dramatic tendencies, these strategies can help create more balanced and harmonious interactions. Remember that dramatic behavior often masks deeper emotional needs, and by approaching it with understanding and compassion, we can foster healthier relationships and personal growth.

Reducing drama in your life

Life is filled with challenges, uncertainties, and inevitable conflicts, but not all of it has to be drenched in drama. In this context, drama refers to excessive emotional reactions, unnecessary conflicts, and heightened tension that can make life more stressful and exhausting than it needs to be. Reducing drama in your life is not about avoiding all challenges or conflicts, but rather about adopting a more balanced and proactive approach to managing them. This section will explore strategies for reducing drama in your life and creating a more peaceful and harmonious existence.

Firstly, it's essential to practice emotional self-regulation. Many instances of drama arise from unchecked emotional reactions. When something triggers intense emotions like anger, frustration, or anxiety, it's easy to react impulsively, adding fuel to the fire. Instead, take a moment to recognize your emotions and their intensity. Mindfulness techniques such as deep breathing or meditation can help you regain emotional control. By managing your reactions, you can prevent minor issues from escalating into dramatic confrontations.

Effective communication is another key to reducing drama in your life. Misunderstandings and miscommunications often lead to unnecessary conflicts. Practice active listening, empathy, and assertiveness to enhance your communication skills. Listen attentively to others, seek to understand their perspective, and express your own thoughts and feelings clearly and respectfully. Open and honest communication can help prevent misunderstandings and reduce the likelihood of conflicts becoming dramatic episodes.

Setting healthy boundaries is crucial in reducing drama. Clear boundaries establish what is acceptable and what is not in your relationships and interactions. Communicate your boundaries assertively and consistently enforce them. For instance, if someone repeatedly crosses a boundary by making hurtful comments, tell them that such behavior is unacceptable and that you expect respectful treatment. Healthy boundaries create a sense of security and stability in your life, reducing the potential for drama.

Another effective strategy is to practice conflict resolution skills. Conflicts are inevitable in life, but they don't have to spiral into dramatic showdowns. Learn how to address conflicts constructively and collaboratively. Avoid blaming, shaming, or escalating the situation. Instead, focus on finding common ground and working together to find solutions. Conflict resolution techniques can help defuse tense situations and lead to more productive outcomes.

Self-awareness plays a significant role in reducing drama. Take the time to reflect on your own patterns of behavior and emotional triggers. Are there situations or people that consistently lead to dramatic reactions? Identifying these triggers can help you prepare and respond more calmly in the future. Additionally, consider seeking feedback from trusted friends or a therapist to gain insights into your behavior and improvement areas.
Simplify your life by minimizing unnecessary stressors. Sometimes, we invite drama into our lives through our choices and commitments. Overcommitting, taking on too many responsibilities, or involving ourselves in toxic relationships can all contribute to a dramatic and stressful existence. Evaluate your priorities and consider where you can streamline your life. Focus on what truly matters to you and let go of the rest. Simplifying your life can lead to greater peace and reduce the potential for drama.

Practice empathy and understanding towards others. Recognize that everyone has their struggles, fears, and insecurities. Empathizing with others can diffuse potentially dramatic situations and foster more compassionate relationships. When you encounter someone who is upset or confrontational, try to understand their perspective and feelings. Offer support and reassurance instead of reacting defensively or with hostility.

Avoid engaging in gossip and drama-inducing behaviors. Gossip can spread like wildfire and escalate conflicts unnecessarily. Refrain from gossiping or spreading rumors, and encourage others to do the same. If you find yourself in a situation where gossip or drama is taking center stage, redirect the conversation to more positive and constructive topics.

Consider the people you surround yourself with. Your social circle has a significant influence on the drama in your life. If you find that specific individuals consistently bring drama into your world, evaluate whether those relationships are worth maintaining. Surround yourself with people who share your values and contribute to a more peaceful and drama-free environment.

Lastly, prioritize self-care. Taking care of your physical and emotional well-being is essential for reducing drama in your life. Engage in activities that bring you joy, relaxation, and balance. Practice self-compassion and permit yourself to rest when needed. A well-rested and emotionally resilient individual is better equipped to handle life's challenges with grace and composure.

In conclusion, reducing drama in your life is not about avoiding all conflicts or challenges but about adopting a more mindful, balanced, and proactive approach to managing them. You can create a more peaceful and harmonious existence by practicing emotional self-regulation, effective communication, setting healthy boundaries, and simplifying your life. Self-awareness, empathy, and a commitment to self-care are crucial in reducing drama and cultivating a life filled with greater tranquility and well-being.

CHAPTER IV

The Control Freak

Characteristics of control freaks

Control freaks are individuals who exhibit a compulsive need to control and manipulate situations, people, and events in their lives. While some degree of control is normal and even necessary for personal and professional success, control freaks take this desire to an extreme, often causing stress, tension, and conflict in their relationships and environments. In this section, we will delve into the characteristics that define control freaks, explore the underlying reasons for their behavior, and discuss the impact they can have on those around them.

One of the primary characteristics of control freaks is their incessant need for control over every aspect of their lives. They feel compelled to micromanage and dictate how things should be done, often displaying rigidity and inflexibility in their approach. Whether it's organizing a social event, managing a project at work, or even dictating how a partner should behave, control freaks want to be in charge of every detail. This desire for control can stem from a need to mitigate anxiety, uncertainty, or a deep-seated fear of failure.

Control freaks are also known for their perfectionist tendencies. They hold themselves and others to impossibly high standards and become distressed when things deviate even slightly from their expectations. This perfectionism can lead to a constant sense of dissatisfaction and frustration for themselves and those who interact with them. In personal relationships, for instance, a control freak may demand perfection from their partner, setting unrealistic expectations that are impossible to meet.

Another hallmark of control freaks is their difficulty delegating tasks or responsibilities. They find it hard to trust others to do things correctly and often believe they can only achieve the desired outcomes. This reluctance to delegate can lead to an overwhelming workload, as control freaks insist on taking on more than they can handle. In a work context, this can result in burnout and hinder collaboration within a team.

Control freaks tend to be highly critical and judgmental of themselves and others. They tend to scrutinize every action and decision, often finding fault even in the smallest of imperfections. This critical nature can be exhausting for those around them, as they constantly feel judged and criticized. In relationships, control freaks may always nitpick their partner's behavior, leading to resentment and strain.

A need for constant reassurance is another common characteristic of control freaks. They seek validation and approval from others to alleviate their anxieties and insecurities. This can manifest in various ways, such as repeatedly seeking affirmation that they are doing a good job, fishing for compliments, or needing constant reassurance of love and affection in personal relationships. This constant need for validation can be draining for those who interact with control freaks, as it often feels like an insatiable demand for attention.

Control freaks tend to be overly rigid and resistant to change. They prefer to stick to routines and established procedures and become anxious when confronted with unexpected situations or deviations from the plan. This rigidity can hinder adaptability and creativity in both personal and professional settings, as they struggle to cope with new challenges or alternative approaches.

Furthermore, control freaks often struggle with communication, particularly regarding listening and compromising. They are more focused on asserting their own ideas and desires rather than truly hearing others' perspectives. This lack of effective communication can lead to conflicts and misunderstandings, as they have difficulty empathizing with the needs and viewpoints of others.

The impact of control freaks on those around them can be significant. Their constant need for control and perfectionism can lead to emotional distance, resentment, and a lack of trust in personal relationships. Partners, family members, and friends may feel stifled and controlled, leading to strained relationships. In professional settings, control freaks can hinder teamwork, as their inability to delegate or adapt to change can stifle creativity and innovation. Their critical and judgmental nature can also create a toxic work environment, affecting morale and productivity.

It's essential to recognize that the behavior of control freaks often stems from underlying fears and insecurities. They may have experienced situations in their past where they felt out of control or vulnerable, leading them to develop coping mechanisms that involve excessive control. Understanding the root causes of their behavior can foster empathy and patience when dealing with control freaks.

In conclusion, control freaks are individuals who exhibit an overwhelming need for control and perfectionism in their lives. Their characteristics include a compulsive desire for control, perfectionism, difficulty in delegating, critical and judgmental tendencies, a need for constant reassurance, resistance to change, and challenges in communication. While their behavior may stem from deep-seated fears and insecurities, it can significantly impact their relationships and environments. Recognizing

for effectively managing boundaries in complex relationships.

When setting boundaries with control-oriented individuals, it's important to acknowledge their perspective and needs as well. While their behavior may be challenging, it often stems from their own fears, insecurities, or past experiences that have led them to develop these control mechanisms. Recognizing their perspective can foster empathy and open the door to more constructive communication.

Setting boundaries with control-oriented individuals can have several positive outcomes. Firstly, it can lead to a more balanced and respectful relationship. When both parties understand and respect each other's boundaries, there is less friction, tension, and conflict. It can also foster a greater sense of personal empowerment and self-esteem. By asserting your boundaries, you affirm your own worth and the importance of your needs and values.

Furthermore, setting boundaries can promote healthier communication and problem-solving within the relationship. When control-oriented individuals understand that they cannot always impose their will, they may be more open to compromise and collaboration. It can also reduce the likelihood of burnout and resentment on your part, as you no longer feel constantly overwhelmed by the demands and control of the other person.

In conclusion, setting boundaries with control-oriented individuals is crucial in maintaining respectful and balanced relationships. It involves self-awareness, clear and assertive communication, consistency, and the recognition of your own needs and the other person's needs. While it may be challenging and may require patience and resilience, the benefits of setting boundaries include improved communication, increased self-esteem, and a healthier and more equitable dynamic in the relationship. Ultimately, boundary setting can lead to greater well-being and satisfaction for both parties.

Finding a balance in control dynamics

Control dynamics exist in all aspects of human interaction, from personal relationships to professional environments. At its core, control is about influence and power, and how it manifests can vary widely. Some individuals lean toward control-oriented behavior, seeking to assert their authority and make decisions, while others prefer a more laid-back approach, allowing others to take the lead. Finding a balance in control dynamics is essential for fostering healthy relationships, maintaining productive work environments, and promoting personal growth. This section will explore the importance of striking this balance, strategies for achieving it, and the benefits it can bring to our lives.

Control dynamics often reflect a power struggle between individuals or groups. Those who lean toward control-oriented behavior may seek to dominate, dictate, or micromanage, while those who prefer a more passive approach may feel disempowered or overshadowed. Finding a balance is about recognizing that power and influence should not be concentrated in the hands of a few but distributed in a way that allows everyone to contribute and thrive.

One fundamental aspect of achieving a balance in control dynamics is communication. Effective communication involves listening, empathy, and assertiveness. Listening allows us to understand others' perspectives, needs, and desires. Empathy helps us recognize the emotions and experiences of others, fostering a sense of connection and understanding. Assertiveness allows us to express our own thoughts, feelings, and boundaries without dominating or being dominated.

To strike a balance in control dynamics, assessing your control tendencies is important. Are you someone who often seeks to take charge and make decisions, or do you tend to defer to others and avoid conflict? Understanding your own control style can help you become more aware of how you contribute to the dynamics in your relationships and environments.

One key strategy for achieving balance is flexibility. Control dynamics should be adaptable to different situations and contexts. In some situations, it may be appropriate for one person to take the lead, while in others, collaboration and shared decision-making may be more effective. Flexibility allows us to adjust our control behavior to suit the situation's needs and the preferences of those involved.

Mutual respect is another vital component of finding a balance in control dynamics. Respect involves valuing the perspectives, contributions, and boundaries of others. It means recognizing that everyone has a role to play and that their input is valuable. Respecting others' autonomy and agency fosters a sense of equality and collaboration.

Recognizing the value of compromise is crucial in achieving a balance in control dynamics. In many situations, a middle ground can be found that allows everyone's needs and preferences to be considered. Compromise may involve making concessions or finding creative solutions that meet the needs of all parties involved. It requires a willingness to let go of rigid control in favor of collaborative decision-making.

Trust is another essential element in control dynamics. Trust involves believing in the competence, integrity, and good intentions of others. When trust exists within a relationship or group, individuals are more willing to share control and delegate responsibilities. Building and maintaining trust requires consistency, honesty, and reliability.

Personal growth and self-awareness are significant in achieving a balanced control dynamic. It involves recognizing our own control triggers, biases, and insecurities. Self-awareness allows us to take a step back, reflect on our behavior, and make conscious choices about how we want to engage with others. It also enables us to let go of the need for excessive control when it hinders our personal growth or the growth of those around us.

Finding a balance in control dynamics brings several benefits to our lives. Personal relationships foster a sense of equality and partnership, where both individuals have a say and contribute to the relationship's growth and well-being. A balanced control dynamic in professional settings promotes teamwork, creativity, and innovation, allowing each team member to leverage their strengths and expertise. It also reduces workplace stress and tension, creating a more harmonious and productive environment.

Moreover, balancing control dynamics can enhance personal growth and development. It encourages us to be more adaptable, empathetic, and open to diverse perspectives. It challenges us to let go of the need for absolute control and embrace collaboration and shared decision-making. It also helps us build stronger, more meaningful relationships with others, as it promotes mutual respect, trust, and understanding.

In conclusion, balancing control dynamics is crucial for fostering healthy relationships, maintaining productive work environments, and promoting personal growth. It involves effective communication, flexibility, mutual respect, compromise, trust, and self-awareness. By striving for this balance, we can create a more harmonious and equitable world where everyone has the opportunity to contribute, collaborate, and thrive. Ultimately, it is a path toward greater connection, fulfillment, and well-being in our lives.

CHAPTER V

The Passive-Aggressive Personality

Identifying passive-aggressive behavior

Passive-aggressive behavior is a common but often misunderstood form of communication and expression of anger or frustration. Unlike overt aggression, which is direct and confrontational, passive-aggression is characterized by indirect and subtle actions or behaviors aimed at achieving a hidden agenda. It can be challenging to identify passive-aggressive behavior, as a facade of politeness or innocence often masks it. In this section, we will explore the key characteristics of passive-aggressive behavior, the underlying reasons for its manifestation, and strategies for recognizing and addressing it in both personal and professional relationships.

One of the most prominent characteristics of passive-aggressive behavior is the expression of negative feelings through non-verbal means or indirect actions. Passive-aggressive individuals may avoid direct confrontation or open communication about their grievances, instead choosing to express their anger or frustration subtly and often covertly. These behaviors can include sarcasm, backhanded compliments, eye-rolling, or other forms of non-verbal communication that convey disapproval or annoyance without actually verbalizing it.

Another hallmark of passive-aggressive behavior is inconsistency. Passive-aggressive individuals may say one thing but do another, creating confusion and frustration for those around them. They might agree to a request or a plan and then intentionally procrastinate, forget, or sabotage it. This inconsistency can lead to a breakdown in trust and undermine the reliability of the individual.

Veiled criticism and hidden agendas are also common in passive-aggressive behavior. Instead of openly expressing their concerns or objections, passive-aggressive individuals may use passive-aggressive language that conceals their true intentions. For example, they might say, "Oh, it's fine. Do whatever you want," when they actually mean the opposite. This indirect approach can be maddening for those trying to understand their true feelings and intentions.

One subtle but telling sign of passive-aggressive behavior is the use of the silent treatment. Instead of engaging in a constructive conversation or addressing issues directly, passive-aggressive individuals may withdraw and refuse to communicate. This tactic is designed to manipulate others into feeling guilty or anxious, often forcing them to apologize or make amends for a perceived offense, even if they are unsure of what they did wrong.

Procrastination and intentional delays are also common passive-aggressive behaviors. When asked to complete a task or meet a deadline, passive-aggressive individuals may drag their feet, make excuses, or intentionally delay progress. This can create frustration and anxiety for those who rely on their cooperation, especially in professional or team settings.

Passive-aggressive individuals may also engage in what is known as "victim mentality." They frequently portray themselves as the innocent party who has been wronged, even when they are the ones responsible for their predicament. This manipulation tactic seeks to garner sympathy and support from others while avoiding responsibility for their actions.

Underlying passive-aggressive behavior are often deep-seated feelings of anger, resentment, or powerlessness. These people might find it difficult to express their feelings honestly because they're afraid of being rejected or confronted. Instead, they resort to passive-aggressive behaviors as a way to indirectly vent their frustrations and regain a sense of control.

Recognizing passive-aggressive behavior can be challenging because it is often subtle and covert. However, there are several strategies to help identify it in personal and professional relationships. First, pay attention to inconsistencies between a person's words and actions. If someone repeatedly agrees to do something but fails to follow through, it may be a sign of passive-aggressive behavior. Likewise, be mindful of non-verbal cues, such as sarcasm or subtle expressions of disapproval, as these can indicate passive-aggressive tendencies.

Communication is key in identifying passive-aggressive behavior. Encourage people to have direct, honest conversations in which they can express their feelings as well as concerns. If someone consistently avoids direct communication and resorts to subtle tactics, it may be a red flag for passive-aggressive behavior.

Trust your instincts. If you feel that someone is being passive-aggressive, take their behavior seriously. Sometimes, individuals may dismiss passive-aggressive actions as harmless, but over time, these behaviors can erode trust and damage relationships.

When dealing with passive-aggressive behavior, it's essential to address it constructively and assertively. Begin by acknowledging the behavior and expressing your feelings about it. Use "I" statements to convey your perspective, such as "I feel frustrated when commitments are not upheld." Encourage open dialogue and invite the individual to share their feelings and concerns as well.

When dealing with passive-aggressive behavior, setting clear boundaries is crucial. Communicate your expectations for respectful and direct communication. Let the individual know that passive-aggressive tactics are not acceptable and will not be tolerated in your interactions.

In some cases, seeking professional help or counseling may be necessary, especially if passive-aggressive behavior is causing significant distress or damage to relationships. A therapist can assist individuals understand the underlying causes of their behavior, develop healthier communication skills, and address unresolved emotions or conflicts.

Addressing passive-aggressive behavior requires patience and empathy. It's essential to recognize that individuals who display such behavior may struggle with their unresolved issues or insecurities. Approaching the situation with understanding and a willingness to work toward more open and direct communication can result in healthier and a more satisfying relationships.

In conclusion, passive-aggressive behavior is characterized by indirect and subtle expressions of negative feelings or hidden agendas. Identifying this behavior involves recognizing its key characteristics, such as non-verbal cues, inconsistency, veiled criticism, and the use of manipulation tactics like the silent treatment or procrastination. Understanding the underlying reasons for passive-aggressive behavior, such as deep-seated anger or resentment, is essential for addressing it effectively. By fostering open and direct communication, setting clear boundaries, and seeking professional help when necessary, individuals can navigate passive-aggressive behavior and promote healthier and more fulfilling relationships.

Dealing with passive-aggressive tactics

Passive-aggressive tactics can be exasperating, confusing, and emotionally draining to deal with in personal and professional relationships. Passive- aggressive behavior involves indirect anger, frustration, or resistance expressions to avoid confrontation or open conflict. Recognizing and addressing these tactics is essential for maintaining healthy and effective communication, resolving conflicts, and preserving the integrity of relationships. In this section, we will explore strategies for dealing with passive-aggressive behavior, its impact on relationships, and the importance of assertive communication.

One of the fundamental strategies for dealing with passive-aggressive tactics is awareness. Recognizing the signs and patterns of passive-aggressive behavior in yourself or others is crucial. Passive-aggressive individuals often avoid direct confrontation and express their negative feelings through subtle actions, non-verbal cues, or veiled criticism. By being aware of these signs, you can start to address them proactively.

Effective communication is a key component of dealing with passive-aggressive tactics. Encourage open and honest dialogue where individuals can express their feelings and concerns directly. In some cases, passive-aggressive behavior may be a response to fear of conflict or rejection, making open communication a critical step in addressing the underlying issues.

Using "I" statements can help facilitate communication in the face of passive-aggressive behavior. Express your own feelings and perspective, focusing on how the behavior affects you. For example, you can say, "I feel hurt when you make sarcastic comments about my work." This approach conveys your emotions without accusing or blaming the other person, which can reduce defensiveness and promote understanding.

Address the behavior, not the person. When confronting passive-aggressive tactics, focus on the specific actions or words that are causing concern, rather than making judgments about the individual's character. Keeping the conversation centered on behavior can prevent the discussion from becoming overly personal or accusatory.

Set clear boundaries for respectful communication. Let the individual know that passive-aggressive tactics are not acceptable in your interactions. Establish expectations for open and direct communication and express your willingness to work together to address any issues that may arise. Boundaries provide a framework for respectful and healthy interactions.

Be empathetic and patient. Recognize that passive-aggressive individuals may have unresolved issues, insecurities, or fears contributing to their behavior. Approach the situation with understanding and a willingness to listen. By demonstrating empathy, you can create a more encouraging and cooperative environment for resolving the underlying problems.

Addressing passive-aggressive behavior often requires persistence. Passive-aggressive individuals may not change their behavior immediately, and it may take time for them to recognize and acknowledge their actions. Be consistent in your efforts to promote open communication and assertive behavior.

When confronting passive-aggressive tactics, it's important to remain calm and composed. Passive-aggressive behavior can be emotionally charged and may provoke strong reactions. Stay focused on the issue at hand and avoid getting drawn into a cycle of defensiveness or aggression. Responding with composure can help de-escalate the situation and promote a more productive conversation.

If necessary, seek professional help or counseling. Dealing with passive-aggressive behavior can be challenging, especially if it is causing significant distress or harm to relationships. A therapist or counselor can provide guidance, strategies, and a safe space for addressing underlying issues and improving communication.

Understanding the impact of passive-aggressive tactics on relationships is crucial for dealing with them effectively. Passive-aggressive behavior can erode trust, undermine effective communication, and lead to frustration and resentment. Personal relationships can create distance and strain, making it difficult to build and maintain intimacy and connection. In professional settings, it can hinder teamwork, collaboration, and productivity, as passive-aggressive behavior often leads to miscommunication and unresolved conflicts. Passive-aggressive tactics can also perpetuate a cycle of negativity and frustration. Conflicts remain unresolved when individuals resort to passive-aggressive behavior instead of addressing issues directly, and resentment festers beneath the surface. This can lead to a toxic and unproductive atmosphere in both personal and professional contexts.

The importance of assertive communication cannot be overstated when dealing with passive-aggressive tactics. Assertiveness involves expressing your needs, feelings, and boundaries directly and respectfully. It allows you to convey your perspective without resorting to passive-aggressive behavior or aggression. Developing assertive communication skills can help break the cycle of passive-aggressive behavior and foster healthier and more effective interactions.

In conclusion, passive-aggressive tactics require awareness, effective communication, empathy, patience, and assertiveness. It is essential to recognize the signs of passive-aggressive behavior, address the behavior rather than the person, set clear boundaries for communication, and approach the situation with empathy and patience. Understanding the impact of passive-aggressive behavior on relationships and the importance of assertive communication are crucial for dealing with these tactics effectively. By promoting open and honest dialogue, individuals can work together to address underlying issues and create healthier and more productive relationships.

Communication strategies to address passive-aggressiveness

Healthy relationships in both the personal and professional spheres are based on effective communication. However, passive-aggressiveness can be a significant hurdle to open and productive communication. Passive-aggressive behavior often involves indirectly expressing negative feelings or resentment, which can create misunderstandings and tension and erode trust. To foster better relationships and resolve conflicts, employing communication strategies that address passive aggressiveness constructively is essential. This section will explore various communication strategies to confront passive-aggressiveness and build more transparent, empathetic, and harmonious interactions.

Passive-aggressiveness is characterized by avoiding direct confrontation, making it a challenge to identify and address. One of the first steps in dealing with passive-aggressiveness is recognizing its signs. Individuals may resort to subtle sarcasm, backhanded compliments, or the silent treatment. They may also employ nonverbal cues like eye-rolling or sighing. By being aware of these signs, one can start to address passive-aggressiveness effectively.

A fundamental strategy in tackling passive-aggressiveness is to promote open and honest dialogue. Promoting direct communication of concerns and feelings can aid in reducing resentment and preventing passive-aggressive conduct. It's critical to provide a secure, accepting environment where people feel at ease discussing their ideas and emotions. Actively listening to what the other person has to say without interrupting or immediately defending oneself is crucial in this context. By fostering open communication, passive-aggressiveness can be replaced with a more direct and constructive exchange of ideas.

Empathy plays a vital role in mitigating passive-aggressiveness. It entails understanding the emotions and perspectives of others, even when they do not express themselves clearly. When confronted with passive-aggressiveness, one can try to empathize with the underlying emotions that drive such behavior. Instead of reacting defensively, one can ask open-ended questions to obtain insight into the other person's feelings and concerns. Acknowledging their emotions and showing empathy makes it easier to address the root causes of passive-aggressiveness and work towards resolution.

Another effective strategy is assertiveness. Assertive communication involves expressing one's needs, feelings, and boundaries clearly and respectfully. It is a balance between passivity and aggression, allowing individuals to communicate their concerns without resorting to passive-aggressive behavior or becoming overly aggressive. Assertive communication can help set expectations and establish boundaries, reducing the likelihood of passive-aggressive responses.

Conflict resolution skills are indispensable when addressing passive-aggressiveness. Instead of allowing conflicts to fester, it is necessary to approach them with a problem-solving mindset. Collaborative problem-solving encourages both parties to work together to find mutually beneficial solutions. It involves identifying the issues, brainstorming possible solutions, and evaluating them objectively. This approach can help transform passive- aggressive behavior into a constructive discussion aimed at resolving the underlying problems.

Additionally, setting clear expectations and boundaries is essential in curbing passive-aggressiveness. When individuals know what is expected of them and the consequences of their actions, they are less likely to resort to passive-aggressive tactics. Establishing open communication channels to discuss expectations and boundaries can prevent misunderstandings and provide a framework for addressing conflicts when they arise.

It is crucial to stay patient and composed when dealing with passive-aggressiveness. Responding with anger or frustration can exacerbate the situation and lead to further resistance. Instead, maintaining a calm and composed demeanor can help de-escalate tensions and encourage the other person to communicate more openly. Patience is especially important when the individual displaying passive-aggressive behavior is not immediately receptive to change.

In some cases, seeking professional help, like counseling or mediation, may be necessary to address deeply ingrained passive-aggressive tendencies. A trained therapist or mediator can facilitate productive discussions and provide guidance on healthier communication patterns. Recognizing when external intervention is needed and being open to it is a sign of maturity and a commitment to improving relationships.

In conclusion, addressing passive-aggressiveness through effective communication strategies is essential for building healthier and more productive relationships. Recognizing the signs of passive-aggressiveness, promoting open dialogue, practicing empathy, and employing assertiveness, conflict resolution, and boundary-setting techniques can reduce passive-aggressive behavior and foster better communication. While it may require patience and effort, the benefits of improved relationships and reduced conflict are well worth the investment in mastering these strategies. Open and honest communication is the key to overcoming passive-aggressiveness and building stronger, more harmonious connections with others.

CHAPTER VI

The Manipulator

How manipulators operate

Manipulation is a complex and often subtle form of influence that individuals may use to control, deceive, or exploit others for personal gain or satisfaction. Understanding how manipulators operate is crucial to recognizing and safeguarding against their tactics. This section delves into the methods and psychology behind manipulation, shedding light on manipulators' various strategies to achieve their objectives.

Manipulators are skilled at exploiting the vulnerabilities and emotions of their targets. They often begin by identifying their victim's weaknesses, insecurities, or desires. These vulnerabilities serve as leverage points, enabling the manipulator to gain a foothold in the victim's psyche. Whether it's exploiting a fear of rejection, a desire for approval, or a need for validation, manipulators use this knowledge to their advantage.

One common tactic employed by manipulators is charm and flattery. They shower their targets with praise, compliments, and attention, creating a sense of trust and admiration. By appealing to the victim's ego and desire for positive feedback, manipulators establish a connection that makes it difficult for the victim to question their intentions. This initial warmth and charisma is a façade that conceals the manipulator's true motives.

Manipulators are skilled at emotional manipulation. They know how to play on their victim's feelings, often using guilt, fear, or sympathy to their advantage. Emotional manipulation may involve creating a sense of obligation or guilt-tripping the victim into complying with their wishes. By invoking strong emotions, manipulators can cloud their victim's judgment and make them more susceptible to manipulation.

Gaslighting is another powerful technique that manipulators use to undermine their victims' sense of reality and self-worth. Gaslighting involves subtly distorting the truth or outright denying facts to make the victim doubt their own perceptions and memories. Over time, victims of gaslighting may become disoriented and lose confidence in their ability to discern the truth. This manipulation tactic erodes the victim's self-esteem and reliance on their own judgment, making them more dependent on the manipulator.

A key aspect of manipulation is the gradual escalation of control. Manipulators often start with small requests or favors, gradually increasing their demands as the victim complies. This incremental approach makes it difficult for the victim to recognize the manipulation until it has reached an unsustainable level. By the time the victim realizes the extent of the manipulation, they may feel trapped or obligated to continue complying.

Isolation is a powerful tool manipulators use to maintain control. By gradually isolating their victims from friends, family, or support networks, manipulators create a situation in which the victim relies solely on them for emotional validation and support. Isolation can make it exceedingly challenging for the victim to seek help or escape the manipulative relationship, as they become increasingly dependent on the manipulator.

Manipulators often employ tactics of deceit and manipulation to cover their tracks and maintain the illusion of trustworthiness. They may lie, fabricate stories, or withhold information to keep their victims in the dark about their true intentions or actions. This web of deception protects the manipulator's interests and perpetuates the cycle of manipulation.

In some cases, manipulators may resort to passive-aggressive behavior, indirect threats, or emotional blackmail to control their victims. By creating an atmosphere of tension and unpredictability, they can manipulate the victim into compliance through fear or anxiety. The victim may feel compelled to avoid conflict or satisfy the manipulator to prevent negative consequences.

Manipulators are often skilled at exploiting the sunk cost fallacy. This fallacy involves the belief that because one has already invested time, energy, or resources into a situation, it is best to continue rather than walk away. Manipulators leverage this psychological bias to keep their victims trapped in toxic or harmful relationships, convincing them that their prior investments would go to waste if they were to leave.

In conclusion, understanding how manipulators operate is essential for recognizing and protecting oneself from their tactics. Manipulation is a complex and multifaceted behavior that relies on exploiting vulnerabilities, charm, emotional manipulation, gaslighting, control escalation, isolation, deception, passive-aggressive tactics, and the manipulation of the sunk cost fallacy. By recognizing these tactics and the psychology behind them, individuals can better equip themselves to detect manipulation, set boundaries, and maintain healthier, more authentic relationships. Vigilance, self-awareness, and willingness to seek support when necessary are essential in safeguarding against manipulators' subtle but damaging influence.

Protecting yourself from manipulation

Manipulation is a pervasive and often insidious aspect of human interaction. It occurs in various forms, from subtle persuasion to outright deception, and can have significant consequences for individuals and their relationships. Protecting oneself from manipulation is crucial for maintaining autonomy, self-esteem, and healthy connections with others. This section will explore the strategies and the techniques that can help individuals safeguard themselves from manipulation and maintain their personal boundaries.

One of the first steps in protecting oneself from manipulation is self-awareness. Being attuned to your own emotions, desires, and boundaries is essential. Knowing what you value and where your limits lie makes it easier to recognize when someone is attempting to manipulate you. Self-awareness also allows you to trust your instincts and intuition, which can serve as early warning systems when manipulation is at play.

Establishing and maintaining healthy boundaries is another key aspect of self-protection. Boundaries are the emotional, physical, and psychological limits you set for yourself in interactions with others. Clearly defining and communicating your boundaries is essential for deterring manipulative individuals who may attempt to cross or manipulate them. Learning to say "no" when necessary and standing firm in your boundaries helps ensure that others respect your autonomy.

Educating yourself about manipulation tactics and psychology is essential for protection. Knowledge is power, and understanding how manipulators operate can greatly improve your ability to recognize and counter their efforts. Familiarize yourself with common manipulation techniques such as guilt-tripping, gaslighting, emotional blackmail, and the exploitation of vulnerabilities. The more you know about these tactics, the better prepared you will be to respond effectively.

Active listening is a valuable tool in protecting yourself from manipulation. Manipulators often rely on miscommunication and misunderstandings to achieve their goals. By actively listening and seeking clarification when needed, you can guarantee that you fully comprehend the intentions and motivations of others. This clarity can help you identify manipulation attempts and respond appropriately.

Maintaining a healthy level of skepticism without becoming overly cynical is another vital aspect of self-protection. While it is crucial to trust others, verifying information and scrutinizing claims that seem too good to be true is equally important. Manipulators often prey on trust and exploit it for their own gain. You can protect yourself from being easily deceived or manipulated by approaching situations with a balanced degree of skepticism.

Building a support network of trusted friends as well as family members is vital in protecting yourself from manipulation. Having people you can confide in and seek advice from can provide an external perspective on potentially manipulative situations. Trusted individuals can offer emotional support, validation, and guidance when you are uncertain about how to respond to manipulation attempts.

Developing emotional intelligence can improve your ability to protect yourself from manipulation. Emotional intelligence entails understanding and managing your own emotions as well as empathizing with the emotions of others. By recognizing your own vulnerabilities and triggers, you can be more resilient in the face of manipulation. Additionally, empathy allows you to better understand the motivations and emotions of manipulative individuals, which can be useful in responding strategically.

Practice assertive communication to protect yourself from manipulation. Assertiveness involves expressing your thoughts, feelings, and needs clearly and respectfully. It enable you to assert your boundaries and stand up for yourself without resorting to aggression or passive compliance. When faced with manipulation attempts, assertive communication lets you express your concerns and assert your boundaries firmly.

Lastly, trust your instincts. If something feels off or you sense that you are being manipulated, don't dismiss these feelings. Your intuition is a valuable tool in self-protection. Take the time to reflect on the situation, seek external perspectives if necessary, and consider distancing yourself from individuals or situations that trigger your instincts.

In conclusion, protecting yourself from manipulation is essential for maintaining your autonomy, self-esteem, and well-being. It involves self-awareness, setting and communicating boundaries, educating yourself about manipulation tactics, active listening, skepticism, building a support network, developing emotional intelligence, practicing assertive communication, and trusting your instincts. By implementing these strategies as well as techniques, individuals can navigate the intricacies of human interaction with greater confidence and resilience, ultimately safeguarding themselves from manipulation and fostering healthier relationships.

Building assertiveness skills

Assertiveness is a crucial communication skill that empowers individuals to express their thoughts, feelings, as well as their needs while respecting the rights and boundaries of others. It stands at the midpoint between passive communication, characterized by compliance and avoidance, and aggressive communication, marked by hostility and dominance. Developing assertiveness skills is essential for fostering healthy relationships, enhancing self-esteem, and navigating various social and professional situations effectively. This section will explore the significance of assertiveness, the benefits of building assertiveness skills, and practical strategies to develop and implement this vital communication skill.

Assertiveness is fundamentally about expressing oneself honestly and respectfully. It involves communicating one's desires, opinions, and boundaries in a way that is clear, direct, and considerate of others. Unlike passive individuals who often yield to the demands of others and avoid conflict, and aggressive individuals who disregard the feelings and needs of others to assert their own, assertive individuals strike a balance. They advocate for their own rights and needs while acknowledging and respecting those of others.

The benefits of building assertiveness skills are multifaceted. First and foremost, assertiveness empowers individuals to have a voice and advocate for their own needs. It helps assert personal boundaries and stand up against mistreatment, manipulation, or undue pressure from others. This self-advocacy is crucial for safeguarding one's self-esteem and maintaining a sense of autonomy.

Assertiveness also contributes to more effective and honest communication. When individuals express themselves clearly and honestly, it reduces the likelihood of misunderstandings and conflicts. Others can better understand their intentions, leading to more productive interactions and healthier relationships. In the workplace, assertiveness is associated with effective leadership, as assertive leaders can provide clear guidance and expectations to their teams.

Moreover, assertiveness fosters self-confidence. As individuals develop and practice assertiveness skills, they build confidence in their capacity to effectively communicate and handle various social situations. This increased self-confidence extends beyond communication and positively impacts other aspects of life, such as decision-making and problem-solving.

Building assertiveness skills requires self-awareness and self-reflection. It begins with recognizing one's communication style and understanding the reasons behind passive or aggressive behavior. Often, individuals may have learned these communication patterns in childhood or through past experiences. Identifying the underlying causes of these behaviors is essential for meaningful change.

One practical strategy for developing assertiveness skills is setting clear and specific goals. Identify specific situations or interactions where you want to be more assertive. This could be in personal relationships, at work, or in social settings. Once you've identified these situations, set clear goals for how you want to respond assertively. For example, suppose you struggle to say "no" to additional work tasks at the office. In that case, your goal might be to assertively decline additional projects while still offering assistance when it aligns with your workload.

Effective communication is at the heart of assertiveness. Learning to express your thoughts, feelings, and needs clearly and directly is essential. Use "I" statements to communicate your perspective and feelings without assigning blame or making judgments. For instance, rather than saying, "You always interrupt me during meetings," you could simply say, "I feel frustrated when I'm interrupted during meetings because it makes it challenging for me to share my ideas."

Another critical aspect of assertiveness is active listening. When others express themselves, make an effort to listen attentively, ask clarifying questions, and show empathy. By demonstrating respect for the perspectives and feelings of others, you foster a more open and collaborative atmosphere.

Practice assertiveness through role-playing or visualization exercises. Imagine challenging scenarios where you would like to respond assertively, and then practice your assertive responses. Role-playing with a trusted friend or therapist can be particularly beneficial, providing a safe environment for honing your skills.

As you work on building assertiveness skills, be patient with yourself. Change takes time, and it is natural to encounter setbacks along the way. Celebrate your successes, no matter how small, and learn from your experiences. Reflect on situations where you successfully applied assertiveness and consider how you can use those strategies in future interactions.

In conclusion, building assertiveness skills is a valuable endeavor that empowers individuals to communicate effectively, advocate for their needs, and maintain healthy relationships. Assertiveness balances passive and aggressive communication, allowing individuals to express themselves honestly while respecting the rights and boundaries of others. The benefits of assertiveness include enhanced self-esteem, improved communication, increased self-confidence, and more effective conflict resolution. To develop assertiveness skills, individuals can set clear goals, practice effective communication, actively listen, engage in role-playing or visualization exercises, and be patient with themselves as they navigate the journey toward assertive communication. Mastering assertiveness can lead to greater self-assurance, improved relationships, and a more fulfilling life.

CHAPTER VII

The Chronic Complainer

Understanding chronic complainers

Chronic complainers seem to be constantly dissatisfied with various aspects of their lives, often expressing their discontent through a consistent stream of complaints. While occasional venting or expressing frustration is a normal part of human interaction, chronic complaining represents a persistent pattern of negativity that can harm the complainer and those around them. In this section, we will delve into the phenomenon of chronic complaining, explore the underlying causes, examine its impact on relationships and well-being, and discuss strategies for dealing with chronic complainers.

Chronic complaining is characterized by repeated dissatisfaction, annoyance, or grievances, often about trivial or inconsequential matters. These individuals habitually focus on the negative aspects of situations, even when there may be positive aspects to consider. Chronic complainers may complain about everything from the weather and traffic to their job, relationships, and health. For them, no aspect of life is immune to criticism.

One key aspect of understanding chronic complainers is recognizing the underlying causes of their behavior. While each individual's reasons for chronic complaining may vary, some common factors contribute to this pattern. One of these factors is a mindset rooted in pessimism or a generally negative outlook on life. Chronic complainers tend to see the glass as half empty, perceiving problems and challenges more readily than opportunities or solutions.

Another factor contributing to chronic complaining is the need for attention and validation. Chronic complainers often seek others' sympathy, empathy, or validation when they express their complaints. They may feel that complaining is a way to connect with others, receive reassurance, or gain a sense of importance. This need for attention can become a habitual and ingrained behavior.

Moreover, chronic complainers may lack effective coping mechanisms for dealing with life's challenges and stressors. Complaining can serve as a coping strategy, allowing them to release built-up tension or frustration. However, this strategy is often counterproductive, perpetuating a cycle of negativity rather than addressing the root causes of dissatisfaction.

The impact of chronic complaining on relationships can be significant. Friends, family members, and chronic complainers' coworkers may feel drained, frustrated, or resentful. Constant exposure to negativity can create a toxic atmosphere and strain interpersonal bonds. Over time, chronic complainers may find that their relationships suffer, as others may distance themselves to protect their own emotional well-being.

In the workplace, chronic complaining can be particularly disruptive. Colleagues and supervisors may perceive chronic complainers as difficult to work with or as obstacles to productivity. This negative perception can hinder career advancement and damage professional reputations. Chronic complainers may also find that their own job satisfaction diminishes, as they focus on dissatisfaction rather than seeking solutions or opportunities for growth.

For the chronic complainer themselves, the habit of constant complaining can take a toll on their mental and emotional well-being. While they may experience temporary relief from venting their frustrations, chronic complaining reinforces a negative mindset and perpetuates feelings of discontent. This can contribute to increased anxiety, stress, and a diminished overall sense of happiness and fulfillment.

Several strategies can be helpful in addressing chronic complaining, both for those who engage in it and those who interact with chronic complainers. For the chronic complainer, self-awareness is key. Recognizing the negative impact of constant complaining on their own well-being and relationships is an essential first step toward change. Developing healthier coping mechanisms, such as mindfulness, stress management techniques, or seeking professional help, can assist in managing dissatisfaction more constructively.

For individuals dealing with chronic complainers, setting boundaries is essential. It's important to express empathy and support but also to communicate when the constant stream of complaints becomes overwhelming or detrimental to the relationship. Encourage the chronic complainer to focus on solutions rather than dwelling on problems, and offer to help them brainstorm ways to address their concerns positively.

Finally, practicing active listening and offering constructive feedback can be valuable. When chronic complainers feel heard and understood, they may be more open to considering alternative perspectives or approaches. You can encourage self-reflection and potentially initiate positive change by gently pointing out the pattern of chronic complaining and its impact.

In conclusion, understanding chronic complainers involves recognizing the underlying causes of their behavior and its impact on both themselves and their relationships. Chronic complaining is often rooted in pessimism, seeking attention and validation, and ineffective coping mechanisms. It can strain relationships and negatively affect mental and emotional well-being. Strategies for addressing chronic complaining include self-awareness, setting boundaries, encouraging a focus on solutions, and practicing active listening and constructive feedback. By addressing chronic complaining constructively, individuals can work toward more positive and fulfilling interactions and cultivate a more optimistic outlook on life.

Responding to constant negativity

Constant negativity can be challenging to deal with, whether coming from a friend, family member, coworker, or even within ourselves. It encompasses a persistent focus on problems, pessimism, and a general outlook that sees the glass as half empty. Responding to constant negativity requires a thoughtful, empathetic approach that balances support with boundaries. This section will explore the impact of constant negativity, strategies for responding effectively, and ways to foster a more positive and constructive environment.

Constant negativity can manifest in various ways, such as chronic complaining, pessimistic thinking, and a tendency to highlight the negative aspects of situations. Individuals who exhibit constant negativity may find it difficult to see the silver lining in any circumstance, and their outlook can affect those around them. The impact of constant negativity can be pervasive, leading to emotional exhaustion, strained relationships, and a general sense of negativity in the environment.

Developing empathy and understanding is one of the first steps in responding to constant negativity. It's essential to recognize that individuals exhibiting constant negativity may be struggling with their own challenges, stressors, or past experiences that influence their outlook. By understanding the root causes of their negativity, you can approach them with compassion and patience, rather than judgment or frustration.

Active listening is a valuable tool when responding to constant negativity. Let the person talk about their feelings and ideas without interfering. A genuine interest in their viewpoint can be demonstrated by posing open-ended queries and requesting clarification. Apart from providing a secure space for them to communicate their concerns, active listening could also reveal more serious issues that are underlying their negativity.

Another important strategy is setting clear and respectful boundaries. While offering support and empathy is important, it is equally essential to maintain your own emotional well-being. If the constant negativity is taking a toll on your mental health or creating an unhealthy dynamic, it's acceptable to set limits on the amount of time and energy you invest in the relationship. Communicate your boundaries respectfully and assertively, emphasizing the need for a more balanced and positive interaction.

Encourage a shift from problem-focused to solution-focused thinking. Individuals exhibiting constant negativity often become stuck in a cycle of dwelling on problems without actively seeking solutions. You can help them redirect their thinking by gently suggesting alternative perspectives or brainstorming possible solutions to their concerns. This can foster a more proactive and constructive approach to challenges.

Model positive thinking and behavior. Your own attitude and outlook can have a significant influence on the people around you. People can be motivated to adopt a more optimistic outlook by exhibiting resilience in the face of adversity and maintaining a positive attitude. Lead by example and show that finding solutions and focusing on the positive aspects of life is possible.

Encourage self-awareness and self-reflection. Help the individual recognize the impact of their constant negativity on themselves and those around them. Engage in open, honest, and non-confrontational conversations about the effects of their behavior on relationships and overall well-being. Encourage them to navigating the underlying causes of their negativity and consider seeking professional help if necessary.

Finally, practice patience and consistency in your approach. Changing entrenched patterns of constant negativity takes time, and there may be setbacks along the way. Be patient with the individual and with yourself as you work towards a more positive and constructive interaction. Consistently reinforce the importance of adopting a more balanced and optimistic outlook.

In conclusion, responding to constant negativity requires a compassionate, balanced approach that combines empathy and boundaries. Recognize that individuals exhibiting constant negativity may have their own challenges and stressors influencing their outlook. Actively listen, set boundaries when necessary, encourage solution-focused thinking, model positivity, promote self-awareness, and practice patience and consistency in your interactions. By responding to constant negativity with understanding and support, you can foster a more positive and constructive environment for yourself and those around you. Ultimately, promoting a shift toward a more optimistic outlook benefits individuals and the relationships and communities of which they are a part.

Encouraging positive change in complainers

Complaining is a common human behavior that allows individuals to express dissatisfaction, frustration, or concerns about various aspects of life. However, when complaining becomes chronic or overly negative, it can impact both the complainer and those around them.

Encouraging positive change in complainers involves fostering self-awareness, promoting healthier communication, and supporting a shift towards a more constructive and optimistic outlook. This section will explore the reasons behind chronic complaining, its effects on individuals and relationships, and strategies for helping complainers embrace a more positive perspective.

Chronic complainers often have underlying reasons for their behavior. Understanding these motivations is a crucial first step in encouraging positive change. Complaining can serve as a coping mechanism, allowing individuals to release stress and frustration. It may also be a way to seek attention, validation, or connection with others. By recognizing the underlying causes of chronic complaining, we can approach the individual with empathy and understanding rather than judgment.

Active listening plays a pivotal role in encouraging positive change in complainers. When individuals feel heard and understood, they are more likely to be open to considering alternative perspectives. Listen attentively to the complainer's concerns, ask clarifying questions, and show empathy. By demonstrating that their thoughts and feelings matter, you create a supportive environment for change.

Encouraging self-awareness is essential for complainers to recognize the impact of their behavior on themselves and those around them. Gently guide them to reflect on how their constant complaints affect their well-being, relationships, and overall happiness. Help them understand that chronic complaining can perpetuate a cycle of negativity, making it difficult to find solutions or experience positive moments.

Promote solution-focused thinking. Chronic complainers often get stuck in a pattern of dwelling on problems without actively seeking solutions. Encourage them to shift their perspective by gently suggesting alternative viewpoints or brainstorming possible solutions to their concerns. By focusing on finding resolutions, they can break free from the cycle of chronic negativity.

Model positivity and resilience. Your own attitude and behavior can serve as a powerful influence on complainers. Maintain a positive outlook and demonstrate how to handle challenges with optimism and resilience. Your example can inspire them to adopt a more positive perspective and learn healthier ways of coping with life's difficulties.

Offer constructive feedback. Engage in open, honest, and non-confrontational conversations about the effects of chronic complaining on relationships and overall well-being. Provide feedback that highlights the importance of a more balanced and optimistic outlook. Encourage complainers to consider the impact of their behavior on themselves and others.

Set boundaries when necessary. While offering support and empathy is essential, it is equally crucial to maintain your own emotional well-being. Suppose the constant complaining is taking a toll on your mental health or creating an unhealthy dynamic. In that case, it is acceptable to set limits on the amount of time and energy you invest in the relationship. Communicate your boundaries kindly but assertively, emphasizing the need for a more balanced and positive interaction.

Practice patience and consistency. Changing entrenched patterns of chronic complaining takes time and effort. Be patient with the complainer and yourself as you work together toward positive change. Reinforce the importance of adopting a more optimistic outlook consistently. Celebrate small victories and progress, no matter how incremental they may be.

In conclusion, encouraging positive change in complainers involves understanding the underlying reasons for their behavior, active listening, promoting self-awareness, fostering solution-focused thinking, modeling positivity, offering constructive feedback, setting boundaries, and practicing patience and consistency. By approaching chronic complainers with empathy and support, we can help them shift towards a more constructive and optimistic perspective. Ultimately, this benefits not only the complainer but also the relationships and communities they are a part of. Encouraging positive change in complainers is a journey towards greater well-being and more harmonious interactions for everyone involved.

CHAPTER VIII

The Victim Mentality

Recognizing victim mentality

Victim mentality, often referred to as a victim mindset or victimhood, is a psychological state in which individuals perceive themselves as constant victims of external circumstances, blaming others or the world for their misfortunes, and feeling helpless or powerless to change their situation. This mindset can be highly detrimental to personal growth, relationships, and overall well-being. Recognizing victim mentality is essential not only for those who may be caught in its grip but also for society as a whole. In this section, we will explore the characteristics of victim mentality, its causes, its consequences, and strategies to overcome it.

Victim mentality is characterized by a consistent pattern of thinking and behavior. Individuals with this mindset often exhibit a tendency to view themselves as perpetual sufferers, believing that life is inherently unfair and that they are always on the receiving end of injustice. They frequently blame others for their problems, refusing to take responsibility for their actions or decisions. This mindset can manifest in different aspects of life, from personal relationships to professional settings.

One common trait of individuals with victim mentality is the belief that they have no control over their lives. They perceive themselves as helpless victims, convinced that external forces or people hold all the power and that they are powerless to change their circumstances. This sense of powerlessness can lead to a defeatist attitude, which further reinforces their victim status.

Another hallmark of victim mentality is the tendency to engage in negative self-talk. Those with this mindset often have a pessimistic outlook on life and habitually focus on the negative aspects of situations. They may engage in self-sabotaging behaviors, such as procrastination or avoidance, due to their belief that they are destined to fail or that their efforts will be futile.

Understanding the causes of victim mentality is crucial in addressing and overcoming it. Several factors can contribute to the development of this mindset. Childhood experiences of neglect, abuse, or trauma can shape a person's perception of themselves as victims. Additionally, societal factors, such as a culture that promotes victimhood or enables dependency, can play a role in reinforcing this mentality. Furthermore, low self-esteem, fear of failure, and a lack of resilience can make individuals more susceptible to adopting a victim mindset. The consequences of victim mentality are far-reaching and can impact different aspects of an individual's life. In personal relationships, those with this mindset often struggle to maintain healthy connections. They may perceive themselves as constantly wronged by their partners or friends, leading to conflict and strained relationships. In the workplace, victim mentality can hinder professional growth, as individuals may avoid taking on challenges or seeking advancement due to their belief that they are destined to fail or be mistreated. This mindset can also lead to a sense of hopelessness and emotional distress, contributing to anxiety and depression.

Recognizing victim mentality in oneself or others is the first step toward addressing it and fostering personal growth. Self-awareness is essential in breaking free from this mindset. Individuals must examine their thought patterns and behavior to identify signs of victimhood. This may involve journaling, seeking therapy, or engaging in introspective exercises that encourage a more positive self-image and a sense of agency.

Changing one's mindset from victimhood to empowerment requires effort and commitment. It entails challenging negative beliefs and replacing them with more constructive ones. Cognitive-behavioral therapy (CBT) is a widely used therapeutic approach that can assist individuals reframe their thoughts and develop healthier coping mechanisms. Building resilience and self-esteem is also crucial, as it empowers individuals to take control of their lives and make positive changes.

In addition to individual efforts, societal changes can play a role in addressing victim mentality. Promoting a culture of personal responsibility and accountability can help reduce the prevalence of this mindset. Encouraging resilience and self-reliance in education and social programs can provide individuals the tools to overcome challenges and setbacks.

In conclusion, recognizing victim mentality is essential for personal growth and societal well-being. It is a mindset characterized by a constant sense of victimhood, blame-shifting, and a belief in one's powerlessness. Understanding the causes and consequences of victim mentality is crucial in addressing it. By fostering self-awareness, challenging negative beliefs, and promoting personal responsibility, individuals and society can work together to overcome the grip of victim mentality and pave the way for more empowered and fulfilling lives.

Supporting individuals stuck in a victim mindset

The victim mindset, characterized by a pervasive belief in one's powerlessness and a tendency to blame external factors for one's problems, can be a challenging psychological state to overcome. Individuals trapped in this mindset often find it difficult to break free from the cycle of negativity and helplessness. Supporting individuals stuck in a victim mindset is a delicate and essential endeavor. In this section, we will explore strategies and approaches to provide assistance and encouragement to those struggling with a victim mentality.

Firstly, it is crucial to approach individuals with a victim mindset with empathy and understanding. Recognizing that their perception of reality may be deeply ingrained and rooted in past experiences is a fundamental starting point. Avoiding judgment and criticism is key to creating a secure as well as non-threatening environment where they can begin to explore their thought patterns and behaviors.

Active listening is an invaluable skill when providing support to those with a victim mindset. Letting them express their thoughts, feelings, and frustrations without interruption or judgment allows them to feel heard and validated. Active listening entails not only hearing their words but also paying attention to their body language and emotional cues. This approach fosters trust and opens the door to productive conversations.

Once a foundation of trust and empathy is established, it is essential to gently challenge their negative beliefs and thought patterns. This can be made by asking open-ended questions that encourage self-reflection and introspection. For example, asking, "What do you think might be another way to approach this situation?" can prompt individuals to consider alternative perspectives and solutions. Encouraging them to explore the underlying reasons of their victim mentality can also be helpful. Often, unresolved past traumas or negative experiences contribute to the development and reinforcement of this mindset.

Supporters should avoid enabling the victim mindset by not indulging in their negative narratives or reinforcing their feelings of helplessness. Instead, they should encourage personal responsibility and accountability. This can be achieved by gently pointing out instances where individuals have agency and control over their choices and actions. Acknowledging their strengths and capabilities can boost their self-esteem and confidence.

Another effective way to support individuals with a victim mindset is to introduce them to positive role models and success stories. Telling the experiences of those who have overcome hardships and accomplished their objectives can instill motivation and hope. Change can be greatly accelerated by realizing that others have gone through comparable struggles and come out stronger. It can also be helpful to encourage people to look for mentors or support groups where they can interact with like-minded people.

Setting goals and creating an action plan are crucial to assisting people in escaping a victim mentality. Collaborating with them to identify achievable goals and steps toward personal growth and change can provide a sense of purpose and direction. Small, incremental successes can build confidence and demonstrate the potential for positive change.

Patience and persistence are key when supporting individuals stuck in a victim mindset. It is important to remember that breaking free from this mindset is a process that may take time. Setbacks and relapses are common, and supporters should be prepared to offer ongoing encouragement and reassurance. Celebrating even small victories along the way can boost motivation and reinforce the idea that change is possible. Encouraging self-care and well-being is another vital aspect of supporting individuals with a victim mentality. Promoting healthy habits, such as regular exercise, mindfulness, and seeking professional guidance when needed, can contribute to overall emotional and psychological well-being. A balanced and nourished body and mind are better equipped to face challenges and cultivate a more resilient mindset.

In some cases, professional help from therapists or counselors may be necessary to address deeply ingrained victim mentality. Mental health experts can offer specialized guidance and therapeutic techniques to help individuals navigate and overcome their negative thought patterns and behaviors.

In conclusion, supporting individuals stuck in a victim mindset requires empathy, active listening, and a patient, non-judgmental approach. Encouraging self-reflection, challenging negative beliefs, and promoting personal responsibility are crucial steps in helping them break free from this mindset. Providing inspiration through positive role models, goal setting, and action planning can motivate individuals to embark on a journey of personal growth as well as empowerment. Ultimately, with the right support and guidance, individuals can transition from a victim mindset to a more positive and resilient outlook on life.

Promoting empowerment and resilience

The victim mentality, characterized by a persistent belief in one's helplessness and a tendency to attribute life's challenges to external factors, can be a limiting and debilitating state of mind. However, it is possible to promote empowerment and resilience in individuals who are trapped in this mindset. By helping them recognize their own agency, build self-esteem, and develop coping strategies, we can support their journey towards a more empowered and resilient outlook on life.

Empowering individuals with a victim mentality begins with fostering self-awareness. Many people with this mindset may not even realize that they are trapped in it. It is essential to gently guide them to recognize their thought patterns and beliefs, which often involve feelings of powerlessness and a tendency to blame others for their problems. This process of self-discovery can be facilitated through open and non-judgmental conversations where individuals are encouraged to explore the origins of their victim mentality.

One of the most significant steps in promoting empowerment is helping individuals take responsibility for their lives. Often, those with a victim mindset tend to avoid responsibility for their actions and decisions, attributing them to external forces. Encouraging them to acknowledge their choices, even in challenging situations, can be a powerful catalyst for change. By highlighting instances where they have control and agency, individuals can gradually reclaim their sense of personal responsibility.

Building self-esteem is another critical aspect of promoting empowerment and resilience. Low self-esteem is often a contributing factor to victim mentality. Therefore, it is essential to help individuals recognize their strengths, talents, and achievements. Encouraging self-compassion and self-acceptance can counteract the negative self-talk that often accompanies this mindset. Supporters should actively challenge negative self-beliefs and replace them with positive affirmations.

Cultivating resilience is another vital component of helping individuals break free from a victim mentality. Resilience is the capability to bounce back from hardship and adapt to challenging situations. To foster resilience, individuals should be encouraged to view setbacks as opportunities for growth rather than as insurmountable obstacles. Promoting a growth mindset, where challenges are seen as learning experiences, can help individuals develop resilience and face adversity with greater confidence.

Goal setting is an effective way to promote empowerment and resilience. Collaborating with individuals to set achievable goals and action plans can provide a sense of direction and purpose. These objectives should be specific, measurable, and realistic, enabling individuals to track their progress and celebrate their achievements along the way. Achieving these milestones can boost self-esteem and reinforce the idea that they have the ability to shape their own destinies.

Support networks are crucial in promoting empowerment and resilience. Individuals should be encouraged to seek out positive and supportive relationships that uplift and motivate them. Family, friends, mentors, as well as support groups can offer valuable encouragement and perspective. These networks can provide a secure space for individuals to share their challenges and triumphs and receive guidance and feedback.

Mindfulness and self-care practices can also contribute to empowerment and resilience. Encouraging individuals to participate in activities that foster well-being, such as meditation, yoga, or journaling, can help them manage stress and establish emotional resilience. These practices enable individuals to stay grounded and centered, even in the face of adversity.

Professional help from therapists or counselors may be necessary in some cases. Mental health professionals are able to provide specialized guidance and therapeutic techniques to help individuals overcome deeply ingrained victim mentality. Cognitive-behavioral therapy (CBT) is one effective approach that can help individuals determine and challenge their negative thought patterns and replace them with a more empowering beliefs.

Ultimately, promoting empowerment and resilience for individuals with a victim mentality requires a multifaceted approach. It involves fostering self-awareness, encouraging personal responsibility, building self-esteem, cultivating resilience, setting goals, nurturing support networks, and embracing mindfulness and self-care practices. It is essential to remember that breaking free from a victim mentality is a process that may take time and effort. Supporters should provide continuous encouragement and support as individuals embark on their journey towards empowerment and resilience. With the proper guidance and determination, individuals can transition from a victim mindset to a more empowered and resilient way of thinking and living.

CHAPTER IX

Difficult People at Work

Dealing with difficult colleagues or bosses

In the professional world, one is bound to encounter challenging colleagues or bosses at some point in their career. Coping with difficult individuals in the workplace is an essential skill that not only contributes to personal well-being but also enhances one's professional growth and success. Such interactions can be emotionally draining and potentially harmful to one's career if not handled correctly. This section aims to provide insights into effective strategies for dealing with difficult colleagues or bosses, emphasizing the importance of communication, self-awareness, empathy, and conflict resolution skills.

First and foremost, communication is the cornerstone of effectively managing difficult workplace relationships. Open and honest communication can help address misunderstandings, clear misconceptions, and create an atmosphere of mutual respect. It is important to express concerns, needs, and boundaries clearly and assertively, avoiding passive-aggressive behavior or bottling up frustrations. When addressing colleagues or bosses about problematic behavior, it is often helpful to use "I" statements, focusing on one's feelings and experiences rather than making accusatory statements. For example, saying, "I feel uncomfortable when you interrupt me during meetings" is more constructive than saying, "You always interrupt me."

Self-awareness is another critical element in dealing with difficult colleagues or bosses. It involves understanding one's emotions, reactions, and triggers in response to challenging situations. By recognizing how certain behaviors or comments affect one's mood and performance, individuals can better manage their emotional responses. Self-awareness allows one to assess whether their reactions are proportionate to the situation and whether they may be contributing to the conflict in any way. Being mindful of one's own biases and prejudices can also help avoid unnecessary conflicts and foster more constructive interactions.

Empathy is a potent tool for resolving conflicts and building better relationships in the workplace. It entails putting oneself in the shoes of the difficult colleague or boss to understand their perspective, motivations, and challenges. While this does not excuse inappropriate behavior, it can shed light on the fundamental causes for their actions. By demonstrating empathy, individuals can create a more supportive and cooperative atmosphere, making it easier to address and resolve conflicts. For example, if a colleague is consistently late for meetings, it may be helpful to inquire about any personal or work-related challenges they are facing that could be causing the issue.

Conflict resolution skills are valuable when dealing with difficult colleagues or bosses. Rather than avoiding conflicts or resorting to confrontation, individuals should strive to resolve issues through constructive dialogue and problem-solving. One effective approach is to use a conflict resolution framework, such as the "I Message" technique or the "Win-Win" method. These methods encourage parties involved in the conflict to actively listen, express their needs and concerns, and work together to find mutually beneficial solutions. It is essential to stay calm, patient, and focused on the issue at hand, staying away from personal attacks or blame-shifting during the resolution process.

Sometimes, seeking assistance from a trusted supervisor, HR department, or a neutral third party can be necessary when dealing with persistent conflicts with colleagues or bosses. These avenues can provide a structured and impartial environment for addressing issues and mediating disputes. Reporting problematic behavior to HR should be done with the aim of finding a fair and constructive resolution, rather than seeking retribution. Maintaining professionalism and confidentiality throughout the process is essential to preserve one's own integrity and reputation.

Another strategy for dealing with difficult colleagues or bosses is to set clear boundaries and expectations. Establishing healthy boundaries helps protect one's well-being and prevents the escalation of conflicts. It is essential to communicate boundaries calmly and assertively, ensuring that they are reasonable and respectful of others' needs and roles. For instance, if a colleague frequently interrupts during work discussions, kindly inform them that you would appreciate uninterrupted speaking time during meetings to ensure effective communication.

Taking care of one's well-being is paramount when dealing with challenging workplace relationships. It is essential to manage stress and emotional reactions through self-care practices, such as mindfulness, exercise, and relaxation techniques. Seeking support from trusted friends, family, or colleagues can provide a valuable outlet for discussing frustrations and gaining perspective. Additionally, keeping a healthy work-life balance can help mitigate the impact of workplace stressors and difficult interactions.

In conclusion, dealing with difficult colleagues or bosses is an inevitable aspect of the professional world. Effective strategies for managing such relationships include open communication, self-awareness, empathy, and conflict resolution skills. It is essential to approach these interactions with a constructive mindset, focusing on finding solutions and maintaining professionalism. By setting boundaries, seeking assistance when necessary, and prioritizing self-care, individuals can navigate challenging workplace relationships with resilience and integrity. Ultimately, these skills not only contribute to personal growth but also create a more harmonious and productive work environment for everyone involved.

Maintaining professionalism in challenging work environments

In the fast-paced and often demanding world of modern workplaces, maintaining professionalism can be a formidable challenge. Difficult colleagues, high-pressure situations, and conflicting priorities can test one's ability to uphold the standards of professionalism. However, professionalism is a crucial aspect of career success and personal growth. It encompasses qualities like integrity, respect, accountability, and adaptability, which not only benefit the individual but also contribute to a positive work environment. This section explores the importance of professionalism in challenging work environments and offers strategies for cultivating and sustaining it.

Professionalism in the workplace goes beyond dressing appropriately or adhering to company policies. It is about consistently demonstrating integrity and ethical behavior, regardless of external pressures or adversities. In challenging work environments, where stress and tension may be commonplace, professionalism becomes even more critical. It sets the tone for the way colleagues interact, influences the company's reputation, and ultimately impacts an individual's career trajectory.

One fundamental aspect of professionalism in challenging work environments is maintaining composure under pressure. When faced with tight deadlines, challenging clients, or stressful situations, it is essential to remain calm and collected. Emotional intelligence plays a significant role here, allowing individuals to manage their emotions and respond effectively to the emotions of others. It is crucial to avoid reacting impulsively or emotionally to challenges, as such reactions can escalate conflicts and hinder problem-solving.

Respect for others is another key component of professionalism in challenging work environments. Treating colleagues, superiors, and subordinates with courtesy and consideration, regardless of the circumstances, is essential. Even when differences arise, professionalism demands that individuals communicate respectfully, listen attentively, and seek common ground. Valuing diversity and demonstrating empathy towards colleagues' perspectives and challenges fosters a harmonious work environment.

Accountability is a hallmark of professionalism, particularly when mistakes or setbacks occur in a challenging work environment. Taking ownership of one's actions, admitting errors, and working towards resolutions demonstrate integrity and responsibility. Rather than shifting blame or avoiding accountability, professionals acknowledge their contributions to a situation and proactively seek solutions. This not only helps resolve issues but also builds trust and credibility among colleagues.

In challenging work environments, adaptability and flexibility are essential professional qualities. Rapid changes in technology, market dynamics, and organizational structures require individuals to embrace change and continuously acquire new skills. Professionals who exhibit a willingness to adapt to new circumstances, learn from challenges, and evolve with the industry are more likely to thrive in demanding workplaces.

Effective communication is a linchpin of professionalism, especially in challenging work environments where miscommunication can exacerbate problems. Clear and concise communication ensures that instructions are understood, expectations are met, and conflicts are resolved constructively. It is vital to listen actively, ask clarifying questions when necessary, and provide feedback in a respectful and constructive manner. Misunderstandings can be minimized, and collaborative solutions can be achieved through effective communication.

Maintaining professionalism in challenging work environments also entails setting boundaries to protect one's well-being. While dedication to one's job is commendable, it should not come at the cost of physical or mental health. Overworking, neglecting self-care, or sacrificing work-life balance can lead to burnout and compromise professionalism. Individuals must establish and communicate their limits, take regular breaks, and seek support when necessary to ensure their continued effectiveness and resilience.

Conflict resolution skills are particularly valuable in challenging work environments. Conflicts are inevitable, but the way they are managed can significantly impact the workplace's atmosphere and productivity. Professionals should approach conflicts with a problem-solving mindset, seeking common ground and solutions rather than escalating disputes. Engaging in constructive dialogue, acknowledging differing perspectives, and involving a neutral mediator when needed can help resolve conflicts professionally.

Networking and building positive relationships within and outside the organization are integral components of professionalism. In challenging work environments, collaborating with colleagues and seeking mentors or allies can provide valuable support and guidance. These relationships can serve as sources of inspiration, professional development, and emotional resilience, helping individuals navigate challenging circumstances more effectively.

Mentoring and leadership also play essential roles in upholding professionalism in challenging work environments. Effective leaders set an example by demonstrating professionalism themselves and fostering a culture of respect and accountability within their teams. Mentoring programs can provide guidance and support to less experienced professionals, helping them develop their professionalism and navigate workplace challenges. In conclusion, maintaining professionalism in challenging work environments is not only a personal responsibility but also a vital contributor to a positive and productive workplace culture. It involves maintaining composure under pressure, showing respect for others, taking accountability, embracing adaptability, and honing effective communication and conflict resolution skills. Professionals must also prioritize their well-being, set boundaries, and seek support when needed to navigate demanding workplaces successfully. By consistently upholding the principles of professionalism, individuals contribute to their own career success and create a more harmonious and resilient work environment for themselves and their colleagues.

Strategies for improving workplace relationships

In the modern professional landscape, success is not solely determined by individual skills and competencies; it is also influenced by the quality of workplace relationships. Building positive relationships with colleagues, supervisors, and subordinates is essential for a productive as well as harmonious work environment.

Effective workplace relationships contribute to job satisfaction, career growth, and overall well-being. This section explores various strategies for improving workplace relationships, emphasizing the importance of communication, empathy, teamwork, conflict resolution, and mutual respect.

Effective communication is one of the foundation of every successful workplace relationship. Clear and open communication fosters understanding, cooperation, and trust among team members. It is vital to actively listen to colleagues, ask clarifying questions when required, and provide feedback in a constructive and respectful manner. Miscommunication can lead to misunderstandings and conflicts, making it crucial to ensure that instructions, expectations, and concerns are communicated clearly and consistently. Encouraging open dialogue and creating a secure space for colleagues to express their thoughts and ideas promotes transparency and strengthens workplace relationships.

Empathy is another essential component of building strong workplace relationships. Empathizing with colleagues involves understanding their feelings, perspectives, and challenges. Taking the time to listen to their concerns and showing genuine interest in their well-being fosters a sense of connection and trust. When individuals feel heard and understood, they are more likely to collaborate effectively and support one another. Empathy also extends to acknowledging and validating colleagues' emotions, even when their viewpoints differ from one's own.

Teamwork plays a fundamental role in workplace relationships, as most professionals collaborate with others to achieve common goals. Building effective teams requires a blend of complementary skills and personalities, but it also hinges on shared values and a dedication to mutual success. Colleagues should be

professional development. Strong workplace relationships contribute to job satisfaction, enhance collaboration, and create a positive work environment. By actively implementing these strategies, individuals can foster more productive, harmonious, and fulfilling relationships with their colleagues, ultimately benefiting both their personal growth and the success of the organization.

CHAPTER X

Difficult People in Personal Relationships

Navigating difficult family members

While a source of love and support for many, family can also be a complex and challenging aspect of our lives. Dealing with difficult family members is a common experience that can test our patience, emotional resilience, and interpersonal skills. Whether it's a confrontational sibling, a critical parent, or a challenging in-law, effectively managing these relationships is essential for maintaining family harmony and one's own well-being. This section will explore strategies for navigating difficult family members, emphasizing communication, setting boundaries, empathy, conflict resolution, and self-care.

Communication is at the heart of any successful relationship, including those with difficult family members. Open and honest communication can help address misunderstandings, clear misconceptions, and create an atmosphere of mutual respect. Expressing concerns, needs, and boundaries clearly and assertively is crucial, avoiding passive-aggressive behavior or bottling up frustrations. When addressing difficult family members about problematic behavior or conflicts, using "I" statements is often helpful, focusing on your feelings and experiences rather than making accusatory statements. This approach can reduce defensiveness and promote more productive conversations.

Setting boundaries is a critical aspect of managing difficult family relationships. Boundaries are essential for defining what is acceptable behavior and what is not. Establishing healthy boundaries helps protect one's emotional well-being and prevent manipulation or emotional abuse. It is important to communicate your boundaries calmly and assertively, ensuring they are reasonable and respectful of both your needs and the other party's needs. While setting boundaries may initially meet resistance, they are essential for keeping a healthy and respectful family dynamic.

Empathy plays a crucial role in navigating difficult family members. It involves understanding their perspective, motivations, and challenges, even when you disagree with them or find their behavior problematic. Empathizing with difficult family members does not mean condoning or accepting their behavior, but it can help you approach the situation with greater understanding and compassion. It may involve considering their past experiences, personal struggles, or insecurities that may be influencing their actions.

Conflict resolution skills are valuable when dealing with challenging family members. Conflicts are a natural part of any relationship and are not necessarily harmful. The key is how conflicts are managed and resolved. When disagreements arise, it is essential to deal with them with a problem-solving mindset rather than an adversarial one. Engaging in constructive dialogue, actively listening, and seeking common ground are effective strategies for resolving conflicts. Avoiding escalation and focusing on solutions rather than blame can lead to more positive outcomes.

Self-care is essential when navigating difficult family members. Dealing with challenging relationships can be emotionally draining and stressful, so it's crucial to prioritize your well-being. This implicates setting aside time for activities that bring you joy and relaxation, seeking help from friends or a therapist, and practicing stress management techniques such as mindfulness or meditation. Keeping a healthy work-life balance and taking breaks when needed are also vital for preserving your emotional and mental health.

It is important to remember that you cannot control the behavior of difficult family members; you can only control your own responses and reactions. Avoid the temptation to change or fix them, as this can result in frustration and disappointment. Instead, concentrate on managing your own emotions and setting boundaries to protect yourself. It may also be helpful to seek support from other family members or trusted friends who can offer perspective and encouragement.

Another strategy for navigating difficult family members is to choose your battles wisely. Not every disagreement or issue requires confrontation or conflict. Assess the situation and consider whether engaging in a potentially contentious discussion is worthwhile. Sometimes, it may be more productive to let minor issues go to preserve family harmony. Save your energy and emotional resources for situations that truly matter.

Seeking professional help, like from a family therapy or counseling, can be a invaluable resource when dealing with particularly challenging family dynamics. A professional therapist can provide guidance, facilitate communication, and offer strategies for improving family relationships. Family therapy sessions can create a safe and structured environment for addressing deep-seated issues and finding constructive solutions.

In conclusion, navigating difficult family members is a common challenge that requires patience, empathy, and effective communication. Setting boundaries, practicing conflict resolution, prioritizing self-care, and choosing your battles wisely are all essential strategies for managing these relationships. While changing difficult family members may not always be possible, you can control your responses and actions. Maintaining your emotional well-being and seeking support when needed can create healthier and more manageable family dynamics that contribute to your overall happiness and peace.

Handling difficult friends or partners

Friendships and romantic partnerships are central to our lives, providing companionship, support, and a sense of connection. However, like any relationship, they can also present challenges when dealing with difficult friends or partners. Difficult friends may exhibit behaviors such as manipulation or insensitivity, while challenging partners may display traits like jealousy or communication issues. Learning how to handle this situations is crucial for maintaining healthy relationships and personal well-being. This section will explore strategies for managing difficult friends or partners, emphasizing effective communication, setting boundaries, empathy, conflict resolution, and self-care.

Effective communication is the foundation of every successful relationship, including those with difficult friends or partners. Open and honest communication can help address misunderstandings, clear misconceptions, and create an atmosphere of mutual respect. When dealing with difficult friends or partners, expressing concerns, needs, and boundaries clearly and assertively is essential. Using "I" statements to concentrate on your feelings and experiences, rather than making accusatory statements, can reduce defensiveness and promote more productive conversations. Creating a safe and non-judgmental space for open dialogue is essential for resolving issues and improving understanding.

Setting boundaries is a critical aspect of managing difficult relationships. Boundaries are essential for defining what is acceptable behavior and what is not. Establishing healthy boundaries helps protect your emotional well- being and prevent manipulation or emotional abuse. When setting boundaries with difficult friends or partners, communicate them calmly and assertively, ensuring they are reasonable and respectful of your needs and the other person's needs. While setting boundaries may initially meet resistance, they are essential for keeping a healthy and respectful relationship.

Empathy is a potent tool when dealing with difficult friends or partners. It involves understanding their perspective, motivations, and challenges, even when you disagree with them or find their behavior problematic. Empathizing with difficult individuals does not mean condoning or accepting their behavior, but it can help you approach the situation with greater understanding and compassion. It may involve considering their past experiences, personal struggles, or insecurities that may be influencing their actions.

Conflict resolution skills are invaluable when managing difficult relationships. Conflicts are a natural part of any relationship and are not necessarily harmful. The key is how conflicts are managed and resolved. When disagreements arise, it is important to approach them with a problem-solving mindset rather than an adversarial one. Engaging in constructive dialogue, actively listening, and seeking common ground are effective strategies for resolving conflicts. Avoiding escalation and focusing on solutions rather than blame can lead to more positive outcomes.

Self-care is essential when dealing with difficult friends or partners. Managing challenging relationships can be emotionally draining and stressful, so it's crucial to prioritize your well-being. This involves setting aside time for activities that bring you joy as well as relaxation, seeking help from friends or a therapist, and practicing stress management techniques like mindfulness or meditation. Keeping a healthy work-life balance and taking breaks when needed are also vital for preserving your emotional and mental health.

Remember that you cannot change the behavior of difficult friends or partners; you can only control your own responses and reactions. Avoid the temptation to try to fix or rescue them, as this can lead to frustration and disappointment. Instead, concentrate on managing your own emotions and setting boundaries to protect yourself. Seek support from other friends or professionals who can offer perspective and guidance.

Choosing your battles wisely is another valuable strategy when dealing with difficult friends or partners. Not every disagreement or issue requires confrontation or conflict. Assess the situation and consider whether engaging in a potentially contentious discussion is worthwhile. Sometimes, it may be more productive to let minor issues go to preserve the relationship. Save your energy and emotional resources for situations that truly matter.

In cases where difficulties persist and significantly impact your well-being, seeking professional help may be necessary. Individual counseling or therapy can provide guidance and support for managing challenging relationships. A therapist can help you navigate your reactions and relationship patterns, develop coping strategies, and decide on the best course of action for your personal growth and well-being.

In conclusion, handling difficult friends or partners requires patience, effective communication, empathy, and boundaries. Conflict resolution skills, self-care, and choosing your battles wisely are also essential strategies for managing these relationships. While it may not always be possible to change difficult individuals, you can control your own responses and actions. You can navigate challenging relationships with greater resilience and personal growth by maintaining your emotional well-being and seeking support when needed. Ultimately, these skills contribute to healthier and more fulfilling connections in your life.

Strengthening personal relationships through communication

Personal relationships are a fundamental aspect of our lives, contributing to our emotional well-being, happiness, and sense of connection. Effective communication is the lifeblood of these relationships, whether they are with family members, romantic partners, friends, or colleagues. Strong personal relationships are built on trust, understanding, and mutual support, all of which rely heavily on clear and empathetic communication. In this section, we will explore the importance of communication in strengthening personal relationships and provide strategies for enhancing the quality of communication within these connections.

In interpersonal relationships, trust is developed and maintained through effective communication. All healthy relationships are created on a foundation of trust. People show transparency and dependability—two attributes necessary for gaining and preserving trust—when they speak honestly and openly with one another. People who trust one another can share their thoughts and feelings, be vulnerable with one another, and rely on one another for emotional support. It is the glue that holds personal relationships together.

One crucial aspect of effective communication in personal relationships is active listening. Active listening involves fully engaging with the speaker, paying close attention to their words, tone, and body language, and seeking to comprehend their perspective. It means being present in the moment and setting aside distractions or preconceived notions. Active listening sends a powerful message that the speaker's thoughts and feelings are valued and respected, which in turn strengthens the bond between individuals.

Empathy is another essential component of communication in personal relationships. Empathy involves listening to the speaker and trying to understand their emotions and experiences from their point of view. It requires putting oneself in the other person's shoes and validating their feelings, even if you do not agree with their perspective. Empathy fosters a sense of connection and support, as individuals feel heard and understood by those they are communicating with.

Clarity and honesty are fundamental principles of effective communication. Being clear and honest in your communication with others helps avoid misunderstandings and prevents conflicts from escalating. Clearly expressing your thoughts, needs, and expectations while also being receptive to the same from others establishes a foundation of trust and understanding. Even when discussing difficult or sensitive topics, honesty is essential for maintaining the authenticity of personal relationships.

Conflict resolution skills are vital for handling disagreements and challenges within personal relationships. Conflicts are unavoidable in any relationship, but the way they are managed and resolved can significantly impact the relationship's strength and longevity. Effective conflict resolution involves addressing the issue directly, listening to each other's perspectives, and seeking common ground. It requires empathy, patience, and a focus on finding solutions rather than winning arguments. Successfully resolving conflicts through communication can lead to increased trust and mutual respect.

Effective communication also plays a role in setting and respecting boundaries within personal relationships. Boundaries are essential for defining acceptable behavior and maintaining personal autonomy and well-being. Clearly communicating your boundaries as well as respecting those of others helps prevent misunderstandings and conflicts. It fosters a sense of respect for each other's individuality and needs. Healthy boundaries create a space where both individuals can feel safe and comfortable within the relationship.

Appreciation and gratitude are often overlooked but powerful communication elements in personal relationships. Expressing appreciation as well as gratitude for the people in your life can strengthen the bond between you and enhance their sense of value and importance. Small gestures, such as thanking someone for their support or acknowledging their contributions, can go a long way in building positive and lasting relationships. Cultivating a culture of appreciation within a relationship reinforces the connection and mutual respect.

Personal relationships also benefit from regular and intentional communication. In today's busy world, it is easy to become caught up in daily routines and responsibilities, neglecting the need for meaningful communication. Setting aside dedicated time for conversations, whether through face-to-face interactions, phone calls, or written messages, helps maintain the connection and ensures that both individuals remain engaged in each other's lives. Frequent communication facilitates the sharing of experiences and emotions and strengthens the connection between people.

In conclusion, effective communication is important in building stronger interpersonal bonds. Trust, understanding, empathy, and conflict resolution are all essential components of communication that contribute to the quality of personal connections. By actively listening, being clear and honest, respecting boundaries, and expressing appreciation, individuals can foster healthier, more meaningful, and longer-lasting relationships. Strong personal relationships are not only a source of happiness and support but also contribute to personal growth and well-being, making effective communication a valuable skill to cultivate and nurture throughout life.

CHAPTER XI

Self-Care and Boundaries

The role of self-care in dealing with difficult people

Dealing with difficult people is an inevitable part of life, whether it's in the workplace, within our families, or in social settings. These individuals can test our patience, emotional resilience, and interpersonal skills. While effective communication and conflict resolution strategies are essential tools for managing challenging relationships, self-care plays an equally crucial role. Self-care is known as the practice of deliberately taking care of one's physical, mental, and emotional well-being. In this section, we will explore the significant role of self-care in dealing with difficult people, emphasizing its impact on emotional resilience, boundaries, empathy, and overall well-being.

Emotional resilience is a key benefit of self-care when facing difficult people. Interactions with challenging individuals can be emotionally draining and stressful, leaving us feeling overwhelmed and depleted. Engaging in self-care practices helps build emotional resilience, enabling us to bounce back from these draining encounters more effectively. Regular self-care activities, such as mindfulness, meditation, or journaling, provide an emotional reset button, allowing us to process our feelings, gain perspective, and regain our emotional equilibrium. Developing this resilience empowers us to navigate challenging relationships with greater composure and a healthier emotional state.

Self-care also plays a crucial role in establishing and maintaining boundaries when dealing with difficult people. Boundaries are essential for protecting our emotional and mental well-being, ensuring that we do not become enmeshed or overly affected by the behaviors and emotions of challenging individuals. Self-care practices can include setting aside time for self-reflection to identify our own limits and needs. It involves asserting our boundaries assertively and respectfully, even when faced with resistance. By consistently practicing self-care and respecting our own boundaries, we send a clear message to difficult individuals about the level of interaction we are comfortable with, promoting healthier and more respectful relationships.

Empathy is another area where self-care can significantly impact our interactions with difficult people. Empathy entails understanding and relating to the feelings and experiences of others. When we engage in self-care and prioritize our emotional well-being, we are better equipped to extend empathy to difficult individuals. By tending to our own needs and emotional state, we create the emotional space to acknowledge and validate the emotions as well as experiences of others, even when they are challenging. Self-care helps prevent burnout and compassion fatigue, allowing us to approach challenging relationships more empathetically and compassionately. Self-care practices also contribute to our overall well-being, which, in turn, enhances our ability to manage difficult people. Taking care of our physical health by means of exercise, proper nutrition, and adequate sleep provides us with the physical energy and resilience needed to navigate challenging interactions. Engaging in hobbies as well as activities that bring joy and relaxation can boost our emotional well-being, providing a counterbalance to the stressors presented by difficult individuals. By prioritizing our overall well-being through self-care, we equip ourselves with the emotional and physical resources necessary to handle challenging relationships more effectively.

One important aspect of self-care in dealing with difficult people is setting healthy boundaries for our emotional involvement. Difficult individuals may engage in behaviors that trigger strong emotional responses, such as anger, frustration, or sadness. Engaging in self-care helps us manage and process these emotions constructively. Activities including deep breathing exercises, meditation, or journaling can help us control our emotional responses and prevent emotional escalation in challenging interactions. This emotional regulation enable us to respond to difficult people with greater composure and a more balanced emotional state.

Moreover, self-care can provide valuable coping mechanisms for managing the stress and emotional toll that often accompany challenging relationships. Stress management techniques, like yoga, mindfulness, or regular exercise, can help alleviate the physical and emotional strain caused by difficult people. Self-care also offers an opportunity for self-reflection, allowing us to gain insights into our own triggers and emotional responses in these relationships. By understanding our own emotional reactions, we can develop healthier coping strategies that promote resilience and emotional well-being.

In conclusion, self-care is a crucial element in dealing with difficult people. It enhances emotional resilience, helps establish and maintain healthy boundaries, promotes empathy, and contributes to overall well-being. Engaging in self-care practices empowers us to manage the emotional toll of challenging relationships more effectively, reducing stress and burnout. By prioritizing self-care, we equip ourselves with the resources and emotional strength necessary to navigate these relationships with composure, empathy, and healthier boundaries. Ultimately, self-care is essential for maintaining our well-being and preserving our mental and emotional health when faced with difficult people in various aspects of life.

Setting healthy boundaries

Boundaries are the invisible lines that describe the limits of what we're willing to accept or tolerate in our relationships, be it with friends, family, colleagues, or romantic partners. Setting healthy boundaries is a key element of self-care and personal well-being. It involves identifying our emotional and physical limits, communicating them assertively, and enforcing them consistently. In this section we will explore the importance of setting healthy boundaries in different aspects of life and discuss strategies for doing so effectively.

Healthy boundaries are essential for maintaining our emotional and mental well-being. They serve as protective barriers that prevent others from overstepping, manipulating, or taking advantage of us. Without these boundaries, we risk becoming emotionally drained, stressed, or resentful in our relationships. For example, setting a boundary in a friendship may mean expressing that you need some personal space and alone time occasionally to recharge, rather than feeling obligated to socialize constantly. A romantic relationship could involve communicating that certain behaviors or comments are hurtful and unacceptable.

Boundaries are also significant in maintaining our physical well-being. They help safeguard our personal space, time, and energy. Setting boundaries in the workplace, for instance, might involve establishing limits on working hours to maintain a healthy work-life balance. In family dynamics, it could mean respectfully declining requests for financial assistance beyond what you can comfortably provide. These physical boundaries protect our physical health and prevent us from feeling overwhelmed by external demands.

Effective communication is key to setting as well as maintaining healthy boundaries. It requires assertiveness, honesty, and clarity. When establishing a boundary, it is important to express your needs and limits directly and respectfully. Using "I" statements can be valuable in this regard, as it allows you to express your feelings and needs without making accusatory statements. For example, saying, "I need some time alone to recharge," is more constructive than saying, "You're always suffocating me."

Consistency is another crucial element of maintaining healthy boundaries. Once you've communicated your boundaries, enforcing them is essential. Inconsistent boundaries can lead to confusion and frustration for both you and the people in your life. When you consistently uphold your boundaries, others learn to respect them, and your relationships become more balanced and respectful.

Setting boundaries also requires self-awareness. To establish effective boundaries, you must understand your needs, limits, and values. This self-awareness enables you to identify when a boundary is necessary and what it should look like. For example, if you value your personal space, you'll be more likely to set boundaries around your need for alone time.

It's important to remember that setting boundaries is not about being rigid or inflexible. Healthy boundaries are adaptable and responsive to the specific circumstances of each relationship. They can evolve over time as your needs and circumstances change. For instance, the boundaries you set with a new romantic partner may differ from those with a long-term friend.

Moreover, it's crucial to recognize that setting boundaries is an act of self-care, not selfishness. It's about valuing and respecting yourself, which, in turn, allows you to have healthier and more respectful relationships with others. Setting boundaries doesn't mean you don't care about others' needs or feelings; it means you prioritize your own well-being while considering the needs and feelings of others.

In some cases, especially when dealing with individuals who consistently disregard your boundaries, it may be necessary to reinforce your boundaries with consequences. For example, if a colleague repeatedly interrupts your work, despite your polite requests to stop, you may need to escalate the matter to a supervisor or HR department. Enforcing boundaries in this way is not about punishment but about reinforcing the importance of respecting your limits.

Setting healthy boundaries also involves being mindful of potential guilt or anxiety that may arise when asserting yourself. It's common to feel guilty when saying no or setting limits, particularly if you are used to accommodating others' needs at your own expense. Remember that guilt is a natural emotion, but it doesn't necessarily indicate that you are doing something wrong. In fact, it often means that you are taking positive steps toward self-care.

In conclusion, setting healthy boundaries is a fundamental aspect of self-care and personal well-being. It protects our emotional and physical health, maintains balanced relationships, and fosters self-respect. Effective communication, consistency, self-awareness, and an understanding of the importance of boundaries are key to establishing and maintaining them. By setting and enforcing healthy boundaries, we prioritize our own well-being, which ultimately enables us to engage in more fulfilling and respectful relationships with others.

Maintaining your emotional well-being

A vital component of overall health and life satisfaction is emotional well-being. It encompasses the ability to determine, understand, and manage our emotions effectively, even in the face of life's challenges and stressors. Maintaining emotional well-being is not only about feeling good; it also impacts our physical health, relationships, and productivity. In this section, we will explore the importance of emotional well-being, the factors that influence it, and strategies for nurturing and maintaining it.

There is more to emotional well-being than simply not feeling bad; it involves a balance of both positive and negative feelings. It's about having the capacity to experience joy, gratitude, and contentment, while also acknowledging and managing feelings of sadness, anger, or stress in a healthy way. Emotional well-being allows individuals to navigate life's ups and downs with resilience and adaptability, rather than being overwhelmed by their emotions.

Several factors influence our emotional well-being, including genetics, life experiences, environment, and daily habits. While genetics can play a role in our predisposition to certain emotional responses, our life experiences and environment have a significant impact. Traumatic events, chronic stress, and adverse childhood experiences can all contribute to emotional distress. On the other hand, supportive relationships, a positive work environment, and a healthy lifestyle can enhance emotional well-being.

One of the key factors in keeping emotional well-being is self-awareness. Self-awareness entails recognizing and understanding our own emotions, as well as the factors that trigger them. It also includes being mindful of our emotional reactions and their impact on our thoughts, behaviors, and relationships. Self-awareness allows us to identify patterns of emotional response and make conscious choices about how to manage and express our feelings.

Emotional regulation is another essential aspect of emotional well-being. It involves the ability to manage and modulate our emotional responses effectively. This means looking for healthy ways to cope with stress, anxiety, anger, and other challenging emotions. Strategies for emotional regulation may include mindfulness meditation, deep breathing exercises, physical activity, or seeking support from a therapist or counselor. By developing these skills, individuals can prevent emotional distress from spiraling out of control.

Maintaining emotional well-being also requires building healthy relationships and seeking social support. Positive social connections provide a source of emotional validation, understanding, and comfort. Gaining perspective on our emotions and experiencing catharsis can come from confiding our thoughts and feelings to close friends or family members. Strong social connections also lessen feelings of loneliness and isolation by acting as a safety net during difficult times.

Effective stress management is essential to emotional health. Prolonged stress can harm our mental as well as physical well-being and have a negative impact on our emotional state. Stress management techniques such as time management, prioritization, and relaxation exercises can help individuals mitigate the negative effects of stress. Additionally, keeping a healthy work-life balance and seeking professional support when needed are crucial for managing stress and preserving emotional well-being.

Practicing self-care is another essential strategy for nurturing emotional well-being. Self-care involves making intentional choices that prioritize our emotional and mental health. This may entail engaging in activities that bring joy and relaxation, such as hobbies, creative pursuits, or spending time in nature. Adequate sleep, proper nutrition, and a regular physical activity also play a significant role in emotional well-being. Self-care is not selfish; it is a necessary investment in our overall health and happiness.

Cultivating a positive mindset and exercising gratitude can have a profound impact on emotional well-being. Focusing on positive aspects of life as well as expressing gratitude for the good things can shift our perspective and enhance our emotional resilience. By cultivating optimism and reframing negative thoughts, individuals can navigate challenges with greater positivity and emotional strength.

Setting healthy boundaries is a key aspect of emotional well-being, as it helps protect our emotional and mental space. Establishing boundaries in relationships, work, and other areas of life allows us to prioritize our well-being and avoid emotional exhaustion or burnout. Communicating our boundaries assertively and respecting the boundaries of others fosters healthier and more respectful interactions.

Lastly, seeking professional help when needed is a sign of strength, not weakness. A therapist or counselor can offer helpful support and guidance for managing emotional challenges, developing coping strategies, and fostering emotional well-being. They can help individuals navigate issues such as anxiety, depression, trauma, or grief and provide tools for enhancing emotional resilience.

In conclusion, maintaining emotional well-being is a vital aspect of overall health and life satisfaction. It involves self-awareness, emotional regulation, building healthy relationships, managing stress, practicing self-care, cultivating a positive mindset, setting boundaries, and seeking professional help when required. By prioritizing emotional well-being, individuals can experience greater resilience, happiness, and fulfillment, even in the face of life's challenges. Ultimately, emotional well-being empowers us to lead more fulfilling and meaningful lives.

CHAPTER XII

Conflict Resolution and Communication

Effective communication techniques

Communication is fundamental to human interaction, shaping our relationships, influencing our decisions, and connecting us with the world. The ability to communicate effectively can have a big impact on both our personal and professional life. It entails having the capacity to actively and sympathetically listen while also being able to communicate ideas, thoughts, and emotions in a clear and thorough manner. This section will examine the value of good communication, go over important methods for enhancing it, and emphasize how applicable it is in different situations.

It takes effective communication to establish and preserve wholesome relationships. In personal relationships, it fosters understanding, empathy, and trust. In the workplace, it supports collaboration, teamwork, and productivity. Effective communication is also vital in resolving conflicts, making educated decisions, and achieving personal and professional goals. Whether it's expressing affection to a loved one, presenting a proposal to colleagues, or negotiating a business deal, effective communication is the key to success.

One of the fundamental techniques for effective communication is active listening. Active listening includes giving your full attention to the speaker, focusing on their words, tone, and body language, and seeking to comprehend their perspective. It means setting aside distractions, such as smartphones or internal thoughts, and being fully present in the moment. Active listening sends a powerful message that the speaker's thoughts and feelings are valued and respected. It allows for better comprehension of the message and helps prevent misunderstandings.

Clear and concise communication is another crucial technique for effective communication. Clarity means expressing your ideas, thoughts, and intentions in a straightforward and understandable manner. It involves choosing words carefully, avoiding jargon or overly complex language, and structuring your message logically. Conciseness means delivering your message in a succinct and efficient way, without unnecessary elaboration. Clear and concise communication guarantees that your message is easily comprehensible and minimizes the risk of misinterpretation.

Empathy is significant in effective communication. Empathy involves understanding and validating the emotions and experiences of others. It means recognizing and acknowledging their feelings, even when their viewpoint differs from your own. Empathetic communication creates a sense of connection and trust, as individuals feel heard and understood. It is particularly important in sensitive or emotional conversations, where validating someone's emotions can deescalate tension and facilitate understanding.

Effective communication also involves nonverbal cues, such as body language and facial expressions. These nonverbal signals can convey emotions and intentions even more powerfully than words. Being aware of your own nonverbal communication and paying attention to the nonverbal cues of others can improve the overall efficiency of your communication. For example, maintaining eye contact, using open and approachable body language, and mirroring the emotions of the speaker can improve the quality of your interactions.

In addition to active listening and also clear expression, asking questions is a valuable technique in effective communication. Asking open-ended questions encourages conversation and invites the speaker to share more about their thoughts as well as feelings. It demonstrates curiosity and a genuine interest in the other person's perspective. Asking clarifying questions when needed helps ensure that you have fully understood the message and can prevent misunderstandings or assumptions.

Tailoring your communication to your audience is essential for effective communication. Various people have different communication styles, preferences, and needs. Adapting your communication to meet these differences can improve the quality of your interactions. For example, speaking more formally in a professional setting, using simple language when addressing children, or adjusting your tone to match the emotional state of the other person can make your communication more effective.

Feedback is an essential component of effective communication, as it guarantees that the message has been received and understood as intended. Providing constructive feedback involves offering specific and actionable information to the speaker. It helps clarify any points of confusion or misunderstanding and encourages ongoing dialogue. Soliciting feedback from others about your own communication can also be valuable for improving your skills and making adjustments as needed.

In conclusion, effective communication is a crucial skill that influences our personal and professional relationships, decision-making, and overall success. Key techniques for improving communication include active listening, clear and concise expression, empathy, attention to nonverbal cues, asking questions, tailoring communication to the audience, providing feedback, and adapting to the communication style of others. By honing these skills, individuals can improve their ability to convey ideas, connect with others, and achieve their goals, ultimately leading to more meaningful and successful interactions in all aspects of life.

Steps to resolve conflicts with difficult individuals

Conflict is an inherent and inevitable part of human interaction, and it can arise in various aspects of our lives, including in relationships, the workplace, and social settings. Dealing with difficult individuals during conflicts can be particularly challenging, as their behaviors and communication styles may exacerbate the situation. However, resolving conflicts with difficult people is possible with the right approach and strategies. In this section, we will discuss steps to effectively resolve conflicts with difficult individuals, emphasizing communication, empathy, problem-solving, and self-care.

The first step in resolving conflicts with difficult individuals is to initiate open and constructive communication. Communication is the foundation for conflict resolution, and it is essential to create a safe and respectful space for dialogue. It is crucial to express your concerns, feelings, and perspective calmly and assertively, avoiding confrontational or aggressive language. Encourage the difficult person to share their viewpoint as well, and actively listen to their side of the story. Effective communication requires giving each other the opportunity to be heard and understood.

Empathy is significant in resolving conflicts with difficult individuals. Empathizing with their emotions and perspective, even when you disagree with them, can foster understanding and connection. Empathy entails placing yourself in their shoes and acknowledging their feelings, even if they are challenging or uncomfortable. When difficult individuals feel heard and understood, they are more likely to be open to finding common ground and resolving the conflict.

Problem-solving is the next crucial step in conflict resolution. Instead of dwelling on past grievances or assigning blame, focus on looking for a solution to the current issue. Collaboratively explore possible solutions with the difficult individual, considering the demands and concerns of both parties. Be willing to compromise and make concessions when necessary to reach a mutually acceptable resolution. Effective problem-solving requires a willingness to work together toward a solution rather than engaging in a power struggle.

Establishing boundaries is another important step in resolving conflicts with difficult individuals. Boundaries are essential for defining acceptable behavior and preventing further conflict. Communicate your boundaries calmly and assertively, ensuring they are reasonable and respectful of both your needs and the needs of the other person. Boundaries help protect your emotional well-being and prevent manipulation or emotional abuse. When difficult individuals recognize and respect your boundaries, it contributes to a more respectful and healthier relationship.

Patience and persistence are virtues when dealing with difficult individuals in conflict resolution. It may take time for both parties to fully understand each other's perspectives and work toward a resolution. Avoid the temptation to rush the process or force an immediate resolution, as this can escalate tensions. Be patient and persistent in your efforts to communicate, empathize, and find a solution. Sometimes, multiple conversations may be necessary to address the underlying issues and reach a meaningful resolution.

Self-care is an often overlooked but essential step in conflict resolution with difficult individuals. Dealing with challenging individual can be emotionally draining and stressful. Prioritize your well-being by practicing self-care techniques such as mindfulness, meditation, or relaxation exercises. Take breaks when needed to manage your emotional state and prevent burnout. Seeking help from friends or a therapist can also be beneficial for processing your emotions and gaining perspective on the situation.

In other cases, involving a neutral third party, like a mediator or counselor, can facilitate conflict resolution with difficult individuals. Mediation provides a structured and impartial environment for communication and problem-solving. A trained mediator can help guide the conversation, keep it focused on the issues at hand, and ensure that both parties have an opportunity to express themselves. Mediation is particularly effective when there is a history of unresolved conflicts or when communication has broken down.

The final step in resolving conflicts with difficult individuals is to maintain open lines of communication and monitor the progress of the resolution. After reaching an agreement, it is essential to follow up and ensure that both parties are holding up their end of the bargain. Establish a system for regular check-ins to assess how well the resolution is working and make adjustments as needed. Open and ongoing communication helps prevent conflicts from reemerging and contributes to the long-term health of the relationship.

In conclusion, resolving conflicts with difficult individuals requires effective communication, empathy, problem-solving, boundary-setting, patience, self-care, and, in some cases, third-party mediation. Conflict is a natural part of human interaction, but with the right approach and strategies, conflicts can be resolved in a way that it strengthens relationships and promotes mutual understanding. By actively engaging in conflict resolution and prioritizing the well-being of all parties involved, it is possible to navigate challenging situations with difficult individuals and move toward more harmonious and productive relationships.

Building bridges and finding common ground

In a world marked by diversity and differing perspectives, the ability to build bridges and find common ground is essential for fostering understanding, resolving conflicts, and promoting unity. Whether in personal relationships, workplaces, or the broader society, bridging divides and seeking common ground enables individuals and groups to collaborate, compromise, and coexist harmoniously. In this section, we will explore the significance of building bridges and finding common ground, discuss key strategies for doing so effectively, and highlight its relevance in various contexts.

Building bridges and finding common ground is paramount in today's polarized and interconnected world. It acknowledges the existence of differences in opinions, beliefs, values, and backgrounds while emphasizing the importance of seeking areas of agreement and cooperation. By doing so, individuals and groups can transcend divisions, build trust, and work toward shared goals, whether it's in politics, religion, culture, or everyday interactions.

One crucial strategy for building bridges and finding common ground is active and empathetic listening. This involves giving genuine attention to the perspectives and concerns of others, even when they differ from your own. Active listening requires setting aside preconceived notions and judgments, asking clarifying questions, and striving to understand the underlying emotions and motivations of the speaker. Empathy, or the ability to recognize and validate others' feelings and experiences, is an integral part of active listening. It fosters connection and opens the door to finding common ground.

Seeking common ground also entails finding shared values or interests that can serve as a basis for cooperation. While individuals or groups may hold differing beliefs or opinions, they often have overlapping interests or concerns. Identifying these commonalities can provide a foundation for collaboration. For example, in a workplace with diverse team members, the shared goal of achieving company success can serve as a unifying factor, allowing individuals to work together despite differing approaches or ideas.

Open and respectful communication is another essential element in building bridges and finding common ground. Expressing one's thoughts and ideas clearly and constructively, while also being receptive to feedback and differing viewpoints, promotes mutual understanding and trust. When individuals feel heard and respected, they are more inclined to engage in productive dialogue and seek areas of agreement. Respectful communication acknowledges the dignity and worth of each person involved, regardless of their differences.

The ability to compromise is a key strategy for finding common ground. Compromise involves making concessions or finding middle ground between differing positions or interests. It requires a willingness to give up some aspects of one's position in order to achieve a mutually acceptable outcome. Compromise is often a pragmatic approach to resolving conflicts and reaching agreements, as it allows for the integration of diverse perspectives and needs.

Another effective strategy is reframing the narrative or issue at hand. Sometimes, conflicts arise from differing interpretations or framing of an issue. By examining the underlying assumptions and reframing the problem in a way that highlights shared interests or concerns, individuals can shift the perspective and find common ground. For instance, in political debates, reframing an issue from a polarized stance to one that emphasizes the common goal of improving society can facilitate compromise and collaboration.

Facilitation by a neutral third party can be particularly helpful in complex or highly charged situations. A mediator or facilitator can guide the conversation, maintain a neutral stance, and create a structured and respectful environment for dialogue. Mediation is often used in conflict resolution processes, such as labor disputes, family conflicts, or international negotiations, to help parties find common ground and reach agreements. Building bridges and finding common ground is not always about resolving conflicts; it can also be a proactive approach to preventing conflicts from escalating. By fostering understanding and collaboration early on, individuals and groups can create a more inclusive and harmonious environment. This proactive approach is particularly relevant in diverse communities, organizations, or societies where differences are prevalent.

In conclusion, building bridges and finding common ground is a vital skill for navigating the intricacies of our interconnected world. It emphasizes the importance of understanding and collaborating with individuals and groups who may hold differing perspectives or beliefs. Strategies for achieving this include active and empathetic listening, identifying shared values and interests, open and respectful communication, compromise, reframing issues, and facilitation by neutral third parties. By actively seeking common ground and valuing the diversity of perspectives, individuals and societies can work toward greater understanding, cooperation, and unity. Ultimately, building bridges and finding common ground is not just about resolving conflicts; it is about fostering a more inclusive and harmonious world for all.

CHAPTER XIII

Growing Through Challenges

Personal growth opportunities in dealing with difficult people

Dealing with difficult people is an inevitable part of life, as we encounter various personalities and communication styles in our personal and professional spheres. While it can be challenging and even frustrating, these interactions also present significant opportunities for personal growth and development. Learning to navigate relationships with difficult individuals can enhance our emotional intelligence, resilience, communication skills, and overall self-awareness. In this section, we will explore the personal growth opportunities inherent in dealing with difficult people and discuss how these experiences can lead to positive self-improvement.

One of the primary personal growth opportunities that arise from dealing with difficult people is the development of emotional intelligence. Emotional intelligence is known as the ability to recognize, understand, manage, and effectively use one's own emotions, as well as the emotions of others. Difficult individuals often provoke strong emotional responses, such as frustration, anger, or stress. Learning to manage these emotions and respond to challenging situations with empathy and composure is a valuable skill that can be honed through these interactions. By practicing emotional intelligence, individuals can gain better control over their reactions and maintain their emotional well-being in the face of adversity.

Resilience is another crucial personal growth area that is cultivated through dealing with difficult people. Resilience is the capacity to bounce back from hardship, adapt to change, and keep a positive outlook despite challenges. Interactions with difficult individuals can be emotionally draining and test one's patience and perseverance. Overcoming these challenges requires resilience, as individuals learn to cope with stress, setbacks, and conflicts in a constructive manner. Developing resilience in the face of difficult people not only improves one's ability to navigate challenging relationships but also strengthens their overall mental and emotional well-being.

Effective communication skills are honed when dealing with difficult individuals. These individuals often have unique communication styles or perspectives that may differ significantly from one's own. Learning to communicate effectively with them involves active listening, clear expression, and adaptability. Practicing these skills not only allows individuals to navigate difficult conversations more successfully but also enhances their ability to connect with people of diverse backgrounds and perspectives. Effective communication is a valuable skill in both personal and professional contexts, and dealing with difficult people provides an excellent opportunity to refine it.

Dealing with difficult people can also lead to greater self-awareness. These interactions often trigger strong emotional reactions and can reveal underlying patterns of behavior or triggers in oneself. By reflecting on these reactions and seeking to understand the reasons behind them, individuals can gain insights into their own vulnerabilities, biases, and areas for personal growth. Self-awareness is the first step toward personal development, as it allows individuals to identify areas where they can make positive changes and improve their overall well-being.

Another personal growth opportunity that arises from dealing with difficult people is the development of patience and empathy. Patience involves the ability to remain calm and composed in the face of frustration or adversity, while empathy entails understanding and validating the emotions and experiences of others. Dealing with difficult people often requires individuals to practice patience and empathy, as it can be challenging to remain understanding and composed when faced with challenging behaviors or attitudes. These qualities are valuable not only in dealing with difficult individuals but also in fostering healthier and more empathetic relationships with all people.

Building assertiveness is another aspect of personal growth that can be cultivated through interactions with difficult individuals. Assertiveness involves expressing one's needs, thoughts, and boundaries in a respectful and clear manner. Dealing with difficult people often necessitates assertiveness to establish boundaries, communicate expectations, and assert one's rights without resorting to aggression or passivity. Learning to be assertive in a respectful way contributes to healthier communication and more equitable relationships.

Lastly, personal growth opportunities in dealing with difficult people include the chance to practice conflict resolution skills. Conflicts are inherent in these interactions, and successfully resolving them requires effective conflict resolution techniques. These skills involve listening actively, seeking compromise, managing emotions, and finding mutually beneficial solutions. Conflict resolution is a vital life skill that can result in a more harmonious relationships and improved problem-solving abilities.

In conclusion, while dealing with difficult people can be challenging and frustrating, it also offers significant opportunities for personal growth and development.

These interactions can enhance emotional intelligence, resilience, communication skills, self-awareness, patience, empathy, assertiveness, and conflict resolution abilities. By embracing these opportunities for growth, individuals can not only navigate difficult relationships more effectively but also cultivate a more profound understanding of themselves and others, ultimately leading to greater personal development and well-being.

Developing empathy and understanding

Empathy and understanding are two important qualities that enable individuals to interact with others on a more profound level, build strong relationships, and navigate the complexities of the human experience. Empathy involves the capacity to recognize and share the feelings and perspectives of others, while understanding encompasses the capacity to comprehend and appreciate different viewpoints and experiences. Both of these qualities are integral to fostering compassion, tolerance, and harmonious interactions in our personal and professional lives. In this section, we will explore the significance of developing empathy and understanding, discuss strategies for cultivating these qualities, and highlight their relevance in various contexts.

Empathy is a key component of emotional intelligence and is crucial in our interactions with others. It involves putting ourselves in another person's shoes, understanding their emotions, and responding with care and compassion. Empathy is not limited to sharing positive emotions; it extends to recognizing and validating negative feelings as well. Developing empathy allows individuals to connect with others on a deeper emotional level, offering comfort, support, and a sense of belonging.

One strategy for cultivating empathy is active listening. Active listening entails giving full attention to the speaker, focusing on their words, tone, and body language, and seeking to understand their perspective. It means setting aside distractions, such as smartphones or internal thoughts, and being fully present in the moment. Active listening sends a powerful message that the speaker's thoughts and feelings are valued and respected. It allows for better comprehension of the message and helps prevent misunderstandings.

Another key aspect of developing empathy is practicing perspective-taking. Perspective-taking requires individuals to imagine themselves in another person's position and consider how they would feel and react in that situation. It encourages a shift from one's own viewpoint to that of the other person, promoting understanding and empathy. Perspective-taking is particularly valuable in situations where individuals may have different cultural backgrounds, experiences, or worldviews, as it helps bridge gaps in understanding.

Cultivating empathy also involves self-awareness. Self-awareness enable individuals to recognize their own emotions, biases, and triggers, which can impact their ability to empathize with others. By understanding their own emotional responses, individuals can better manage their reactions and remain open and empathetic toward others, even in challenging situations. Self-awareness is a key element of emotional intelligence and supports the development of empathy.

Understanding, on the other hand, involves the cognitive aspect of empathy. It entails comprehending different viewpoints, beliefs, and perspectives, even if they differ from one's own. Developing understanding requires an open and curious mindset, a willingness to learn from others, and the ability to consider alternative viewpoints without judgment. It also involves recognizing the complexity of human experiences and acknowledging that there is often more than one valid perspective.

One effective strategy for cultivating understanding is education and exposure to diverse perspectives. This can involve reading books, attending lectures, or engaging in conversations with people from different backgrounds, cultures, or beliefs. Exposure to diverse perspectives broadens one's horizons and challenges preconceived notions, leading to greater understanding and tolerance. It helps individuals recognize the richness and diversity of human experiences.

Promoting open and respectful dialogue is another essential step in developing understanding. Open dialogue boosts individuals to share their thoughts, experiences, and viewpoints in a safe and non-judgmental environment. It fosters meaningful conversations that allow for the exchange of ideas and perspectives. By actively seeking to understand others and engaging in respectful discussions, individuals can broaden their understanding and appreciation of different viewpoints.

Cultivating empathy and understanding is particularly relevant in today's diverse and interconnected world. These qualities are essential for fostering inclusivity, tolerance, and harmonious coexistence in a global society. They are also crucial in resolving conflicts, bridging divides, and promoting empathy on a broader scale, such as in politics, international relations, and social justice movements.

In the workplace, empathy and understanding are vital for effective teamwork, collaboration, and leadership. Leaders who demonstrate empathy and understanding create a more supportive and productive work environment. They are better equipped to address the demands and worries of their team members, leading to improved job satisfaction and performance. Likewise, employees who practice empathy and understanding contribute to a positive workplace culture characterized by mutual respect and cooperation.

In conclusion, developing empathy and understanding is essential for building strong relationships, fostering compassion, and navigating the complexities of human interactions. Strategies for cultivating these qualities include active listening, perspective-taking, self-awareness, exposure to diverse perspectives, and open and respectful dialogue. These qualities are not only valuable in personal relationships but also in broader contexts, such as the workplace, politics, and social justice efforts. By actively developing empathy and understanding, individuals contribute to a more empathetic and harmonious society where differences are respected, and compassion prevails.

Becoming a more resilient and adaptable person

In the face of life's challenges, uncertainties, and setbacks, resilience and adaptability are two qualities that can significantly enhance an individual's ability to thrive and succeed. Resilience is known as the capacity to bounce back from adversity, overcome obstacles, and maintain one's mental and emotional well-being. Adaptability, on the other hand, involves the ability to adjust and thrive in changing circumstances, embracing new situations, and learning from experiences. Both resilience and adaptability are not fixed traits but rather skills that can be developed and honed over time. In this section, we will explore the importance of becoming a more resilient and adaptable person, discuss strategies for cultivating these qualities, and highlight their relevance in various aspects of life.

Resilience plays a pivotal role in an individual's ability to cope with life's challenges and bounce back from setbacks. It involves developing emotional strength, perseverance, and the capacity to stay hopeful in the face of adversity. Resilient individuals find setbacks as opportunities for growth as well as learning rather than insurmountable obstacles. They can withstand stress, maintain their well-being, and continue to pursue their goals even when faced with significant setbacks. Resilience is a valuable asset in navigating personal and professional challenges and is essential for maintaining mental and emotional health.

One strategy for cultivating resilience is developing a growth mindset. A growth mindset is known as the belief that abilities as well as intelligence can be developed through effort, learning, and perseverance. Embracing a growth mindset allows individuals to view failures and setbacks as opportunities for growth as well as improvement, rather than as indications of their limitations. By reframing challenges as learning experiences, individuals can build their resilience and bounce back more effectively from adversity.

Another important aspect of resilience is building a strong support network. Social support from friends, family, and colleagues provides emotional validation, understanding, and encouragement during difficult times. Knowing that one has a support system to turn to can enhance resilience and help individuals cope with stress and adversity. Seeking help and support when required is a sign of strength, not weakness, and is an important part of resilience.

Developing emotional regulation skills is also crucial for resilience. The ability to effectively identify, comprehend, and control one's emotions is known as emotional regulation. It consists of techniques like deep breathing exercises, mindfulness meditation, and cognitive-behavioral methods that assist people in managing anxiety, stress, and other difficult emotions. By developing emotional regulation skills, individuals can prevent emotional distress from spiraling out of control and maintain their resilience in the face of adversity.

Adaptability is another quality that is closely related to resilience but focuses on one's ability to adjust to new circumstances and thrive in changing environments. In today's fast-paced and unpredictable world, adaptability is a highly valuable skill. It involves embracing change, staying open to new experiences, and being ready to learn and grow in different situations. Adaptability allows individuals to navigate transitions and uncertainty with confidence and optimism.

One effective strategy for cultivating adaptability is embracing a growth mindset, as mentioned earlier. A growth mindset not only fosters resilience but also encourages individuals to view change and new experiences as opportunities for learning and personal development. It enables them to approach unfamiliar situations with curiosity and a positive attitude, rather than resistance or fear.

Developing a proactive approach to problem-solving is also essential for adaptability. Proactive problem-solving involves anticipating challenges, seeking solutions, and taking initiative in navigating change. It means being resourceful and flexible in finding solutions to unexpected problems or obstacles. Proactive problem-solving empowers individuals to take control of their circumstances and adapt more effectively to changing environments.

Embracing continuous learning is a crucial aspect of adaptability. Lifelong learning involves a commitment to acquiring new knowledge, skills, and experiences throughout one's life. It enable individuals to stay relevant in a rapidly changing world and adapt to evolving technologies and industries. Lifelong learners are better equipped to thrive in diverse professional settings and seize opportunities for personal growth and career advancement.

Maintaining a growth mindset and practicing self-compassion are also crucial for adaptability. Self-compassion entails treating oneself with kindness as well as understanding, especially in the face of failure or setbacks. It means acknowledging that everyone makes mistakes and faces challenges, and that self-criticism and perfectionism are counterproductive. Cultivating self-compassion allows individuals to bounce back from failures and setbacks with greater resilience and adaptability.

In various aspects of life, including personal relationships, the workplace, and pursuing personal goals, resilience and adaptability are invaluable qualities that empower individuals to thrive in the face of challenges and uncertainty. By developing a growth mindset, building a strong support network, practicing emotional regulation, embracing proactive problem-solving, continuous learning, and self-compassion, individuals can become more resilient and adaptable. These qualities not only enhance one's ability to navigate life's ups and downs but also contribute to overall well-being and personal growth. In a constantly changing world, the ability to bounce back from adversity and thrive in new situations is a valuable asset that can lead to greater success and fulfillment.

CONCLUSION

In "Difficult People Decoded: Insights and Tactics for Improved Interpersonal Relations," we have delved into the intricate world of challenging personalities, offering readers a comprehensive understanding of various difficult personality types and the tools to navigate these complex interactions effectively.

Throughout this book, we explored the characteristics and behaviors of individuals such as narcissists, drama queens, control freaks, manipulators, chronic complainers, and those with a victim mentality. By recognizing these traits and their underlying motivations, readers are better equipped to decipher the dynamics at play in their relationships.

We provided practical strategies and tactics for dealing with difficult people, emphasizing the importance of setting boundaries, practicing empathy, and maintaining self-respect. Whether in personal or professional contexts, these insights can empower individuals to assertively navigate challenging interactions, fostering more harmonious and constructive relationships.

Ultimately, "Difficult People Decoded" serves as a valuable guide for those seeking to improve their interpersonal skills and improve their ability to connect with others. By understanding and effectively dealing with difficult personalities, readers can navigate the complex web of human relationships with greater confidence, empathy, and resilience.

Thank you for buying and reading/ listening to our book. If you found this book useful/ helpful please take a few minutes and leave a review on the platform where you purchased our book. Your feedback matters greatly to us.